AMERICAN EDUCATION APARTHEID—AGAIN?

DARYAO S. KHATRI
ANNE O. HUGHES

A SCARECROWEDUCATION BOOK

The Scarecrow Press, Inc.
Lanham, Maryland, and Oxford
2002

A SCARECROWEDUCATION BOOK

Published in the United States of America
by Scarecrow Press, Inc.
A Member of the Rowman & Littlefield Publishing Group
4720 Boston Way, Lanham, Maryland 20706
www.scarecroweducation.com

PO Box 317
Oxford
OX2 9RU, UK

British Library Cataloguing in Publication Information Available

Library of Congress Cataloging-in-Publication Data

Khatri, Daryao S., 1945–
    American education apartheid—again? / Daryao S. Khatri and Anne O. Hughes.
        p. cm.
"A ScarecrowEducation book."
    ISBN 0-8108-4451-6 (cloth : alk. paper) — ISBN 0-8108-4452-4 (pbk. : alk. paper)
    1. Education—United States. 2. Public schools—United States. I.
Hughes, Anne O. II. Title.
    LA217.2 .K47 2002
    370'.973—dc21   2002005358

♾™ The paper used in this publication meets the minimum requirements of
American National Standard for Information Sciences—Permanence of
Paper for Printed Library Materials, ANSI/NISO Z39.48-1992.
Manufactured in the United States of America.

This book is dedicated to our spouses, Monika Khatri and Jack Hughes, for their tireless support and patience throughout the entire process of writing the book.

CONTENTS

ACKNOWLEDGMENTS

We wish to express our gratitude and appreciation to two persons who contributed significantly to the content and style of this book. First, Jack Hughes, the spouse of Anne Hughes, has been extremely helpful in providing resource advice and material as well as specific suggestions for federal policy inclusions in the book. He has inspired us to document and personalize our successful teaching approaches in the true spirit of "telling it like it is" in reaching and teaching disadvantaged students to succeed in school and life. Second, we acknowledge the meticulous and thoughtful editing of the draft manuscript by Dr. Thomas Oliver, former Chair of the English Department at the University of the District of Columbia.

In addition, we want to recognize and sincerely thank staff members of the Scarecrow Press, Inc.: First, Dr. Tom Koerner, Vice President and Editorial Director, for identifying and supporting the publication of a book arguing that to improve the public schools, we must improve their teachers—and this means their preparation and support; second, Ms. Cindy Thursman, Acquisitions Editor, for effectively walking us through the publication process; and finally, Dr. Joseph L. Eckenrode who labored tirelessly to edit and polish our manuscript.

PROLOGUE

American public education is facing unparalleled challenges. Eliminating the achievement gap between various racial and ethnic groups is the goal of new national legislation. Placing a highly qualified teacher in every classroom is another goal.

As meritorious as these goals are, the realities facing public education make them difficult to attain. A shortage of teachers—of any quality— threatens, as nearly half of the current teacher workforce approaches retirement, and low salaries make the teaching profession less attractive than many other jobs. Further, the percentage of students from poor and minority backgrounds is growing, due to immigration and varying birth rates while the percentage of more advantaged—and higher achieving—students is declining.

How can the nation reconcile the need to improve student achievement with the reality of finding good teachers and effectively educating the growing numbers of less-prepared students?

Drs. Daryao Khatri and Anne Hughes offer some answers. They maintain that good teachers are made, not just born; and teachers can be trained to deal effectively with students from all backgrounds; and that no generation of students ought to be written off.

These are powerful ideas, and the authors' recommendations for implementing them deserve a hearing. The old ways of handling our problems are not relevant to the tremendous challenges facing us today, and new ways may open doors of opportunity to more students.

No proposal reform, however promising, should escape careful analysis and scrutiny. The ideas in this volume, as well as all others, ought to be subjected to thorough evaluations as experimentation occurs. We owe all children a rigorous and fair analysis of any method proposed to improve their education.

Drs. Khatri and Hughes are to be commended. They have clearly seen the challenges facing American education and have come up with some fresh ways of addressing them. Their commitment to those students who are less advantaged shows through in their writing.

The authors' fear of a new apartheid deserves attention. The American vision of a melting pot of all nationalities and races forming to make a common citizenry does not happen by chance. If we want a better and more unified country, we must work to achieve that end, and improving education for all students is a good place to start.

Jack Jennings, Director,
Center on Education Policy

1

INTRODUCTION

What should a school be?

"A school ought to be a magical place where you are queen or king, and where what you get to do is focus on your intellect, and on what you can accomplish as a human being, and you come to understand what your life *can* be. That's what school should be for children . . . . School is supposed to be full of hope, and it's a place where you go to find out how magical your mind is and how terrific it will be when you develop your mind to its full potential."[1]

This answer was given by Ruth Simmons, president of Brown University, based on her personal experience in the 1950s and 1960s in a ghetto public high school in Houston, Texas. Why is this description no longer true of many public schools as we enter the new millennium? Why are so many schools no longer viewed as magical and hope-filled places? Why do we have hopelessly dysfunctional schools, like Chester Public High School in the Chester Upland School District of Pennsylvania? As *The New York Times* has noted

"Chester is known throughout Pennsylvania for illiteracy, gang warfare and an astronomical dropout rate that peaked above 40 percent in the late 1990s. [This district] has performed so disastrously for so long that the state considered dissolving and dispersing the children throughout nearby suburbs—an idea that went nowhere after the suburbs screamed bloody murder."

Nine of Chester's ten schools have been taken over by Edison Schools, Inc., a company specializing in improving dysfunctional schools. But Chester apparently is in a class by itself when it comes to having "a culture of apathy and failure. . . ." The article further points out that "the most daunting problem of all involves the older high school students whose life prospects have been gravely damaged by a system that has failed them, beginning on the very first day of first grade." Among other discoveries made by Edison were that a "significant number" of high school students could not read the textbooks given to them, and a number of other students were "four to six years below grade in reading." Paradoxically, through testing, some students were "found to be years ahead of their classmates but failing, perhaps as a way of fitting in." All were apparently finding ways to "survive by camouflaging their talents."[2] One of the authors observed all these phenomena many years ago in the Woodlawn section of Chicago, right across the Midway, when she was a doctoral candidate at the University of Chicago.

Somehow, much of the public education enterprise has gone from being the much-touted pathway to individual self-realization and the collective good to being an obstacle course for many. Instead, we have statements about public education like this one made by Andy Rooney, a commentator for the television news program *Sixty Minutes:*

> When the president of the United States has a school-age child, the child does not go to a public school in Washington, D.C., because the schools aren't good enough. How did we let this happen? We have money. We find the money to defend ourselves when war is imminent. We should find the money to educate ourselves because this is a war and we are losing it.[3]

Over the past 50 years, the public education enterprise has been increasingly buffeted by a growing number of major problems, which persist despite numerous efforts to fix them by all three levels of government. The funding formulas under current government structures are mind-boggling. The number of political conflicts among the stakeholders in education has increased in the struggle to make the schools work for poor and minority students, which has led to vouchers, charter schools, and lawsuits. And as if these problems in dealing with existing minorities were not enough, the schools are now faced with handling newly arrived immigrants, who enrich racial/ethnic diversity but at the same time provide new challenges. Unfortunately, these challenges have included lower scores on achievement tests and high attrition rates for significant numbers of students at both the secondary and college freshman levels. Governance has become a big issue, and the federal government, a long-time minor partner in education, is beginning to play an increasingly important role, as the fight for equal educational opportunity at all levels intensifies.

Now added into this bubbling cauldron of problems is the looming teacher shortage. The Department of Education estimates that the shortage will reach 2.5 million by the year 2010. An attendant problem is teacher preparation. Colleges of education are succinctly described in the *New York Times* as having "a reputation as the least rigorous branch of undergraduate education" and as spending "too much time on pedagogy and not enough on content."[4]

Ironically, while this reputation of the colleges of education is becoming well known to the general public, another part of the problem has surfaced that is generally *not* recognized by the same public: the enormous complexity of the teaching task. Maryland Montgomery County Education Association President Mark Simon put it well: "[teaching] *is* rocket science."[5] Having worked in ethnically diverse and poverty settings for most of our teaching careers, we can only say, "Amen, brother!"

Major questions now become: What to do? Where to start? What is the process?

Some of the answers are already in place. For example, there is general agreement that early childhood education is terribly important for a child's subsequent academic achievement in school and the adequate socialization of the child. The accruing evidence with regard to Head Start's benefits and other early learning programs clearly attests to the significance of concerted intervention among very young children. If anything, the effort at this level should be intensified, so that all children are included. Lately, another intervention strategy for the public education system has been proposed and has now been enacted into law: additional achievement testing in grades three through eight, in order to increase accountability in public school systems. But where is the teaching to improve student performance—short of teaching the test? Yet, teaching the test, and only doing so, has emerged as a current scandal.

In addition to these interventions, we argue that two other critical areas for intervention only now are coming into public focus. Within the last year or so, high schools have come under intense scrutiny because of the appalling student attrition rates in big cities. A conservative estimate of the general attrition rate at this level is that 40 percent of those entering the ninth grade will not complete high school—now recognized in our society as the minimum requirement to become a productive citizen. What this figure means is that we are throwing away a huge number of the nation's oncoming generation and condemning them to live lives of squalor and unrealized potential, as well as creating burdens for society in the future. In many cases, especially in urban settings, students who leave school come from the "have nots" of the society. These students are really the throwaway kids. We argue that if early childhood education is the first best chance for a child to succeed academically and socially, then secondary education becomes the last and only chance to salvage a child for society.

The other critical area for intervention is the classroom teacher. We further argue that the starting point for rescuing the system must be the teacher in the classroom. The classroom teacher is where "the rubber hits the road" in the educative process. This fact has been well accepted at the early childhood level by the general public, but it has not been accorded the same importance at either the high school level or the first year of college. And it needs to be. At the high school level, teacher under-preparation has surfaced not only in the particular disciplines, such as mathematics and English, but also in a deficient knowledge of increasingly diverse student populations. One of the consequences of the September 11, 2001 terrorist attacks was the spotlight that fell upon some members of American society for their physical and religious characteristics. As a nation, we were suddenly reminded of our diversity as a people, as well as the need to be sensitive to and to understand it. Teachers have a major role to play in developing an understanding and appreciation of diversity in their students, but first they must learn it themselves.

On the one hand, teachers often are maligned for not knowing how to teach or what to teach, and at the same time they are chastised for being ignorant of, insensitive to, or prejudiced towards the racially and culturally diverse students they teach. On the other hand, they are sidestepped or ignored in reform strategies that push equipment, alternative school funding formats (charter schools, vouchers, etc.), back-to-basics "cookbook" reading and math programs that fail to provide the basics, and the latest entry— standardized tests as the primary measure of accountability. In the end, these strategies leave the failing schools and their teachers untouched. The teacher is either the villain in the piece or is spirited out of it altogether. In the former case, the teacher is the problem; in the latter case, overlooking the teacher's role is like leaving Hamlet out of the play.

The truth of the matter is that the problems of the education enterprise from the standpoint of the classroom teacher have not been described, including how tough—and lonely—and underpaid—the job really is. Further compounding the situation is that most new teachers simply are not secure in their content knowledge, are not prepared to handle diverse student populations, and are not adequately mentored in their first year or two of teaching.

The difficulty of the job is attested to by the requests for transfer from "hardship" schools and, in many instances, leaving the profession altogether within the first three years. One of the authors began her career in just such a school.

Both of us have taught at various levels of the public education enterprise. We have conducted teaching-learning experiments during this period with students who have reflected enormous diversity, were usually products of largely dysfunctional schools, and were seriously under prepared. Some of our experiments also involved college faculty who were our peers working with the same kinds of students. Based on our experiences in the teaching profession and a detailed examination of public education, we offer an analysis of the problems and a set of proposals for reform that can go a long way in rescuing the public education system. These proposals for reform include actions that can be taken at all three levels of government and governance.

This book is organized into eight chapters. Chapter 2 presents historical background on problems that have arisen with regard to teaching, poor academic preparation of students, teacher preparation and pay, and the large attrition of students from classes. Chapter 3 addresses the contemporary social context in which the public school system as a frontline agency must carry out its mission. Chapter 4 considers current problems specifically faced by schools with regard to diversity, learning and testing. Chapter 5 deals with the teaching dilemma as we move into the new millennium. Chapter 6 describes the key components of the teaching model with regard to teaching-learning principles and their applications to teacher training, using current computer technology as a new and valuable content area. Included as part of this model are techniques for handling diverse student populations and classroom management. The sixth chapter also presents the case for compressing the traditional time frame accorded to pedagogical training for discipline-qualified professionals into approximately two months. Chapter 7 presents a set of proposals for reform at the three levels of government. Finally, Chapter 8 presents a futuristic scenario of what will happen to public education if substantive reforms are not achieved: American education apartheid—again.

NOTES

1. Frey, J. (2001, March 21). Education's golden door. *The Washington Post,* pp. C1, C3.

2. Staples, B. (2002, March 4). *The New York Times,* p. A26.

3. Rooney, A. (1999). There are dumb teachers too. *Tribune Media Services,* p. 12.

4. Zernike, K. (2000, August 24). Less Training, More Teachers: New Math for Staffing Classes. *The New York Times,* p. A1.

5. Schulte, B. (2000, September 20). New era for struggling teachers. *The Washington Post,* p. B7.

2

HISTORICAL BACKGROUND

As it embarks on a new millennium, the public education enterprise has endured a turbulent century. On the one hand, it has made gains in the inclusion of many racial and ethnic groups, expanded educational opportunities at every level, and gained a clearer understanding of the importance of education in maintaining and furthering a democratic society. On the other hand, the public education enterprise is failing to serve an increasingly diverse population adequately, is facing a severe shortage of trained teachers, and is confronting a rising set of expectations from citizens. In order to address the most pressing problems facing public education at the high school level and during the first year of post-secondary education, we examine public education in the twentieth century as it relates primarily to these two levels.

THE SECONDARY LEVEL

At the beginning of this millennium, public education at the secondary level is facing a major crisis. This is manifest in several phenomena: a national teacher shortage; a growing student population that is increasingly diverse and under prepared and scores low on standardized tests; teacher preparation under challenge; teacher competency under challenge; and an eroding financial base. In this regard, the big cities have been the hardest hit and have been struggling with this combination of problems since the late 1950s. But lately, even the more affluent schools in the suburbs have begun to experience the same problems. The crisis is no longer localized in one segment of our society; all segments are being affected. The general public is criticizing the educational enterprise as not serving the needs of the current student population or of society itself. This was certainly not the case at the beginning of the twentieth century. What has led to this situation?

To understand, we must look back to the period around 1900, when Americans, in general, were proud of their free public schools. Although never described as such—the term came much later, the schools have always been a frontline agency, since they educated young citizens in, and acculturated new immigrants to, American democracy. Teachers were respected and valued members of the community wherever they lived and practiced. The promise of upward mobility offered by the schools was well recognized, but there were problems looming on the horizon. Some of these problems and their historical relevance have been well documented by Diane Ravitch[1] in her book *Left Back*. For example, the demands on public education increased substantially as a result of the rapid industrialization and commercialization of the United States and its steady urbanization. Starting in the 1890s, a "tug-of-war" about what education should provide to its constituents commenced among educational leaders. These issues centered on what kinds of education should be provided and to whom.

One school of thought favored training for jobs and underwriting vocational schools, where the knowledge and skills that students gained could be applied to known situations. Supported by industry and business and aided by the military buildup for World War I, this school of thought gained sufficient momentum and clout to achieve the passage of the *Vocational Education Act of 1917*. High schools in the cities, where rapid industrialization and commercialization were occurring, began to add courses in the trades. In contrast, a second school of thought favored training the mind, the time-honored classical approach, or what has come to be termed *academic education*, where the knowledge and skills that students learn are intended to be applied to a variety of unknown and intellectually challenging situations.

Occurring in the same time frame and further complicating the intellectual tug-of-war were the demands placed on the schools to educate the children of immigrants coming from the eastern and southern parts of Europe. These immigrants came to escape problems in their homelands, find opportunities for work, and achieve a better life in the United States. Although not well educated, they usually had a great respect for education and its benefits. At this time, schools were the social institution charged with the "Americanization" of these immigrants through teaching English, inculcating American civic values and ways of life, and preparing students for gainful employment.

The end of World War I saw the emergence of the United States as a world power and a continuation of the educational tug-of-war. Indeed, tensions became even more intense in the mid-1920s and early 1930s, when a new approach, progressive education or progressivism, entered the fray. Trying to understand the issues involved was the educational philosopher, John Dewey,[2] who basically advocated for a careful examination of "education itself rather than in terms of some 'ism about education, even such an 'ism as 'progressivism'." His warning that the so-called new approach, progressive education or progressivism, should not be confused with vocational education, posed many difficulties in terms of both theoretical conceptions and "modes of practice."[3] The "training of the mind" or classical approach, he called "Traditional Education." While recognizing theoretical conceptions and their contributions to education, Dewey was cognizant of their major weaknesses. Dewey noted that

> [the] trouble with traditional education was not that educators took upon themselves the responsibility for providing an environment. The trouble was that they did not consider the other factor in creating an experience; namely, the powers and purposes of those taught. It was assumed that a certain set of conditions was intrinsically desirable, apart from its [traditional education] ability to evoke a certain quality of response in individuals. This lack of mutual adaptation made the process of teaching and learning accidental. Those to whom the provided conditions were suitable managed to learn. Others got on as best they could. Responsibility for selecting objective conditions carries with it, then, the responsibility for understanding the needs and capacities of the individuals who are learning at a given time.[4]

Throughout his book, *Experience and Education,* Dewey never questioned the importance of content, contrary to how people have interpreted many of his writings. Content is essential. It had to be sequenced properly; it should be predetermined by knowledgeable faculty in school systems, and it must be of value in a particular culture. The trick was to anchor the content selected within the experiences of the learner, in order to maximize the learning experience. As Dewey pointed out, all learning occurs in the present—not in the future; the learner is never passive—even if he is being treated that way. He is always learning something, and it could be to shun the experience associated with confronting the content, a classic case in point being fear of math.

In light of Dewey's assertion about two types of students in the classroom, those for whom learning conditions are suitable and those who "got on as best they could," we define the latter as "limp-along" students, children whom the system gives up on or who simply disappear into the ether as "throwaway kids." All too often, these are minorities and recent immigrants.

Dewey was further concerned that content would be diluted if there was an over-emphasis on teaching methodology. Even then, and contrary to his warnings, many teachers and administrators in colleges of education and school systems diluted course content, overemphasizing the experience of the learner at the sacrifice of what is to be learned. This approach came to be known as "Progressive Education." To the authors of this book, it was just a "bad" translation of Dewey. Unfortunately, this approach and its practices continued well into the latter half of the twentieth century.

But there were other problems, too. Although not widely advertised during the 1920s and 1930s, the average student achievement of local school districts continued to show differences, as was always the case. In general, affluent and well-financed school districts demonstrated consistently solid achievement levels. Rural school districts lagged behind. Beginning at this time, and continuing through the 1940s, big-city school systems began to be impacted by the migration of a large segment of the southern black population to the cities in the North and the increasing drift of the rural population into the cities, looking for jobs.

Further complicating the situation, and also beginning in the 1940s, was the slowly evaporating pool of qualified women who went into teaching. The school administrators had typically paid women sparingly, assuming either they could get away with it or that for most of these women the proceeds from teaching represented the second income in a household. During the years leading up to World War II, the teaching profession at the elementary and secondary levels was dominated by women. It was one of the few professions ungrudgingly open to women. However, many of these women found more lucrative employment in burgeoning industry and government as a result of World War II. This pattern was never reversed, as opportunities continued to open up for women in other professions during the last half of the twentieth century. With the computer revolution of the 1980s and 1990s and the shortage of qualified workers in technological and other fields, women often didn't consider the teaching profession, even when salaries in affluent districts increased. The qualified and the talented teachers who were available typically went to these districts. The big-city and rural school systems had to settle for what they could get. This problem of finding a qualified teaching staff was largely concealed during the 1940s, 1950s and early 1960s because of World War II and postwar priorities.

During the 1950s, the American economy was doing well and with prosperity came the increasing expectations of minorities. The civil rights movement was bubbling up and scored a major triumph with *Brown v. Board of Education* in 1954, the landmark ruling that overturned segregation in the schools of the South. By and large, United States school systems, whether north or south of the Mason-Dixon Line, were unprepared to handle the new social condition, and public attention began to focus on the schools. In 1956, the Russians launched the first satellite, Sputnik, and the schools found themselves under fire for failing to prepare students in math, science and foreign languages. In turn, this problem led to the *National Defense Education Act* of 1957. During this period, the flight of the white population to the suburbs began, a movement that would contribute substantially to a declining tax base for big cities and, when coupled with an industrial decline, would ultimately lead to a number of cities going broke in the 1980s.

In 1960, the nation discovered poverty and discrimination on a large scale. By 1964 and 1965, three seminal pieces of legislation had been passed: the *Civil Rights Act*, the *Economic Opportunity Act* (which included Head Start, deliberately separated from the school systems because of their perceived stultifying influence), and the *Elementary and Secondary Education Act*, which included the now massive and widely accepted *Title I* program that called attention to the special needs of disadvantaged children. While a few school systems did mount innovative programs, most continued to engage in business as usual, and the poverty and minority students continued to lag behind. By the early 1980s, the problem had become so severe that a nationally based commission published a devastating report on the schools entitled *A Nation At Risk*. Math, science, reading and the resultant achievement scores in these areas were all seen to be far below other democratic societies; the public school systems and the teacher education programs seemed to be unable to effect revitalizing changes.

Despite efforts at reform, such as the application of new equipment, mentoring, vouchers, and back-to-basics programs, the situation has remained largely unchanged. Teacher education was coming under increasingly critical scrutiny. Continuing throughout the entire period from 1984 until the present have been such administrative practices as assigning teachers to areas in which they have either limited content expertise (e.g., assigning a biology teacher with one course in physics to teach physics) or hiring new teachers who were largely expected to maintain law and order in the classroom and who often did not have sufficient content knowledge and/or pedagogical training to be effective teachers. Another growing problem faced by big-city and rural school districts was that well-qualified teachers had their choice of teaching positions, and these districts were usually—and still are—the last choice. Only recently are the suburbs running into trouble as well.

Further exacerbating the situation in the late 1980s and the 1990s has been the influx of new immigrants, many of whom have only limited or no English language fluency. At the high school level, the situation has become acute. And the problem of lowered minority performance, particularly among Latinos and African Americans, simply continues. So, it is not surprising that the classroom life of a new teacher has become increasingly short: from three to five years.

Thus, from being viewed as a "can do" vital social institution at the beginning of the 1900's, the public schools have become an out-of-touch, insulated, and often dysfunctional social institution for large numbers of our citizenry at the beginning of the 2000s, and this is particularly true in secondary education. Moreover, teachers have been challenged on a number of levels, such as their preparation in the subject matters they are teaching, their setting of lowered expectations for certain minority groups, principally African Americans and Latinos, and their inability to deal with diversity. Adding to its woes, the education enterprise is facing a severe shortage of 2.5 million teachers, mainly at the secondary level, during the next decade as reported by the U.S. Department of Education. This problem is expected to worsen in the high demand areas of math, science, English, reading and some foreign languages. The belated recognition that the secondary level is in crisis is in contrast to the widespread knowledge of the importance of pre-school education, stemming from the Head Start experience. At the beginning of the twenty-first century, secondary education is suddenly front and center.

Not surprisingly, the problems associated with inadequate preparation of students are surfacing also at the postsecondary level. Initially experienced in the public colleges and universities at the freshman and sophomore levels and in community colleges, these problems have now rippled through much of higher education.

POSTSECONDARY LEVEL: FRESHMAN YEAR

One of the most difficult problems facing higher education institutions is the growing number of underprepared college students, who often drop out. The problem initially began in the late 1960s in public two- and four-year institutions that typically had some variation of an open admission policy. Prompted by the Civil Rights Act, earlier court decisions regarding segregation, and rising expectations among large numbers of African-Americans and older students, new kinds of students entered these institutions in increasing numbers. Most of these new students in higher education were "first generation," and their academic preparation was uneven. By and large, the receiving institutions simply were not prepared for these new kinds of students. While publicly supported higher education did respond by offering developmental or remedial courses in mathematics, reading, and English, these courses basically have not made much of a difference in improving the student retention rate.

Why does this situation continue to exist? The hidden problem here is that in presenting their courses to a changing and non-traditional population, professors generally have persisted in using the "empty-receptacle" approach—pouring knowledge into students who were presumed ready to be filled with it. This approach was usually the method whereby the professorate itself had been educated. Let us put this lack of change on the part of professors in historical perspective.

It is well known in institutions of higher learning that professors in almost all cases are hired to be researchers, and teaching seems to take a back seat. This was definitely the case when we were hired back in the 1960s and 1970s. Our respective academic departments, as is true of most other academic departments of higher education in the country, required that research, publication and securing grants come first, and teaching is basically secondary—one just has to do it. The attitude has been that anyone with content expertise can teach. In spite of these traditional priorities and responsibilities and also because of our employment in a minority institution with an open admissions policy, we became interested in improving the retention rate of our own underprepared and minority students.

Typically, the faculty of higher education institutions have been called upon to solve retention problems within diverse student populations. Additionally, to solve such problems, faculty have often used an approach that identifies the academic deficiencies of the learner. Unfortunately, faculty members have never looked at themselves as being a major part of the problem, as being "deficient." We came to this realization early on in our teaching of non-traditional and minority students. In effect, we as faculty members came to realize that we and our colleagues were perfect illustrations of Pogo's dictum: "we have seen the enemy and he is us."

As we enter the new millennium, the problems continue, and they impact virtually every institution in the country. So what has led to this tremendous increase in the underprepared student population at the postsecondary level?

Prior to World War II, higher education was basically limited to a small, academically well-prepared segment of the population. Typically, this group of students went straight from high school to college without any intervening work experience. Most were in the age cohort of 18 to 22 years of age, and they were largely white. The basic emphasis was on the liberal arts and natural sciences. No emphasis was placed on training professors to teach at this level; a solid knowledge of the discipline was considered to be sufficient, a practice which continues to this day. Professors typically lectured. Also, students were expected to be capable of learning by themselves with rather minimal guidance. And by and large, they were able to do so. If they were unable to learn via the lecture method, they just struggled along or self-selected out of college.

As we noted earlier in this chapter, Dewey's assessment of the teaching/learning roadblock accurately describes the conditions that existed in the 1930s, when higher education was the privilege of a favored elite. However, when Congress threw open the gates to higher education through the GI Bill after World War II, the game rules began to change drastically. A flood of non-traditional students from all walks of life and all ethnic groups crossed the thresholds of our institutions of higher education. Racial equality became a new standard of education following the 1954 *Brown v. Board of Education* ruling of the Supreme Court, and was subsequently reinforced by the *Civil Rights Act* of 1964. Further advancing the opportunities for lower-income students, federal financial aid initiatives of the 1960s and 1970s, including guaranteed student loans, basic educational opportunity (now Pell) grants, work-study and Upward Bound programs, provided the financial means to broaden the student body. As a result, the undergraduate enrollment increased by almost 400 percent from 2.4 million in 1946 to 9.3 million in 2001 as reported by George F. Will.[5]

One major outcome of this explosion in student numbers is that higher education is no longer a privileged right of the chosen few. It is rapidly becoming the birthright of every student who aspires to learn and succeed in life. Another outcome of this explosion in higher education has been that a large segment of the student body is arriving poorly prepared in the academic skills of reading, writing, and computation. These underprepared students pose a challenge of increasing dimensions to those who preside over the classrooms of our colleges and universities.

In the latter half of the twentieth century the faculty in both majority and minority universities by and large, continued to use the same lecture techniques. As a result, the number of those students "who got on as best as they could" or didn't get on at all kept on increasing. In other words, the general teaching technique did not change, and the students kept on dropping out of the academic programs of postsecondary education. In order for many professors to avoid changing their basic teaching technique or to consider themselves as possibly being at fault, the face-saving explanation was to blame the victim—"the student was not prepared." From assertions of this sort, it has been easy for professors to jump to the conclusion that certain students cannot learn the subjects being offered and that such students should be advised to drop the course.

We disagree with this assessment by professors when it is used to justify dropout rates approaching 80 percent. Instead, we conclude professors are unable to utilize the experience base of the students in teaching them. Why do we draw this conclusion? We contend that the professors relied on only the deficit model when evaluating the learner's aspect of the teaching-learning duality. Evidence of the deficit model can be seen in the kinds of proposals we submitted to federal agencies, such as the Department of Education and the National Science Foundation, which have called for new interventions to reduce the attrition rates of non-traditional students, beginning in the 1970s.

One such example is the FIPSE program of the U.S. Department of Education that has actively advocated the use of new techniques for delivering instruction at both the secondary and postsecondary levels. In its guidelines, the problem has been labeled as "teaching and learning". In response to these guidelines, almost all proposals submitted have focused on the learner. Rarely has any proposal submitted dealt with retraining college faculty in the delivery of instruction. We conjecture that the reason for the scarcity of such proposals is because the proposal writers themselves are faculty members and obviously believe they can teach and therefore do not need training and/or retraining in teaching. One exception we know is the University of the District of Columbia's (UDC) Cooperative Education Project, where the emphasis *was* on changing the faculty's style of teaching. Here an effort was made to utilize the students' own experience in relating to a given subject matter. In this model, the instructor was supposed to group the students and serve as a resource person. Unfortunately, freshman and sophomore students didn't have a sufficient knowledge base to really pursue and understand new topics, and participating faculty members found themselves on the sideline with only minimal input. This project was another (belated) example of a bad translation of Dewey.

The aggregated effect of the problems faced by the public education enterprise at both the secondary and postsecondary levels is that now a national crisis exists. First, an increasingly diverse population with a growing number of underprepared students will continue to fill the classrooms, a situation that is not likely to be reversed as a result of rising expectations. The problem we are facing is how to educate this population, not should we educate them. Second, the shortage of teachers, who are trained both in content and pedagogy and who can deal successfully with a culturally diverse population, is upon us. To solve this problem, we must first recognize that a crisis does exist.

NOTES

1. Ravitch, D. (2000). *Left Back.* New York: Simon & Schuster.

2. Dewey, J. (1938). *Experience and Education.* Chicago, Ill.: Kappa Delta Pi.

3. Dewey, J. (1938). *Experience and Education.* Chicago, Ill.: Kappa Delta Pi, p. vi.

4. Dewey, J. (1938). *Experience and Education.* Chicago, Ill.: Kappa Delta Pi, pp. 44–45.

5. Will, G. F. (2001, March 15). The SAT's Thankless Task. *The Washington Post,* p. A25.

3

THE SCHOOLS IN
SOCIETAL CONTEXT

In a paraphrase of John Donne's famous line "no man is an island," so too no public school is an island. Each and every school is part of the "main." Thus, no school reform can ignore the social context in which it must function. In describing the social context, we have included illustrations drawn from our professional experiences in the District of Columbia, its public schools, and its open-admission public university. The authors worked for many years as professors at the University of the District of Columbia and know the District, and particularly that segment of the District's population that is seriously underserved. Moreover, the problems of the D.C. Public Schools are the same as those of other big city school systems. However, the location of the D.C. Public Schools is unique: it sits in the capital of the most powerful nation in the world and is generally rated as one of the worst school systems in the country.

In this chapter, we examine the mission of the schools in the social context of a rapidly changing American society.

A FRONTLINE AGENCY

Whether the schools want to acknowledge it or not, they are a major social institution and, in our view, a frontline agency as well. The characteristics of contemporary society itself require them to function as such. First, the schools always have had the mission of providing formal instruction and guidance in the knowledge, skills, and cultural values necessary for each oncoming generation to become responsible and productive members in the furtherance of American society, its democratic way of life, and its role as a great world power. Second, the schools also have a major responsibility in identifying the talents and needs of individual students and in taking whatever actions are deemed appropriate as part of the continuance of the American society. This mission becomes increasingly important, given the continuing influx of immigrants into the United States.

Third, the society attaches so much importance to this mission that it legally decrees that at specified ages major portions of each individual's time be spent in formally organized educational settings. When one examines a typical day in the life of a student between the ages of six and sixteen, one finds that virtually all but a few waking hours in that day are taken up by school and school-related activities. No other social institution, except the family, is sanctioned to fill so much of a young person's time. And although the family may actually have more of the child's hours, the majority of these hours are spent sleeping, engaging in recreation, or hanging out. Except during the summer months, most of the "prime-time" waking hours of a child belong to the school.

Fourth, the physical placement of the schools in the community is another key to the importance of their mission. No other social institution, with the exception of churches and family homes, is physically located in every part of the community. The school plants are there, including all their equipment, materials and athletic spaces. Unfortunately, much of the schools' time is "down" time; that is, school programs run for approximately eight hours per day five days a week. The schools are physically present on the front line of each community. As such, they are well placed to be a functioning part of the entire community, that is, for all members, not just the school-aged population. What better place could be found than a school to house after-school programs, voter registration, ESL classes, quiet study halls at night, student clubs, adult education, literacy programs, special projects in the community, student parties, and so on?

Finally, the public schools are constantly interacting with a range of members from throughout society: parents, students, boards, politicians, lawyers, and businesspeople. Instead of resisting these interactions, the schools should reach out to involve them constructively in making substantive contributions to school programs. As a frontline agency, the schools must reach out to address the needs of society with the message of, "Look, we need your help and involvement. Become partners with us so we will be better at what we do," instead of, "Go away! Leave us alone. It's not our role." or "Just give us the money. We know what to do."

Unlike society with its changes, the essential mission of the public schools has not basically changed. However, the ways in which this mission plays out have been expanded. Perhaps, more is expected of the schools than ever before, but any attempt to retreat or to build a fortress that ignores elements of our society will inevitably fail. No apologists, like Diane Ravitch, in her book, *Left Back,* can hope to turn the clock back or narrow the mission of the schools.

PUBLIC FUNDING AND POLITICS

The public financing and the politics of education in the United States are a very mixed bag. On one hand, schools located in affluent suburbs or better sections of cities are graduating a large percentage of their student bodies and preparing them well for colleges; these schools are adequately financed and usually have non-partisan political support. On the other hand, schools located in the inner cities of the nation and some of the poorer rural areas, such as Appalachia, are experiencing high attrition rates and preparing few college-bound students. They are receiving only limited funding, much of which must come from the state. As a result, these schools are penalized.

Another aspect of the financial picture is the public sources of funding, federal, state and local. Federal funding of public education still is below the ten percent level of total funds, and state and local units fund the remaining portion in mixed patterns that reflect the political and economic conditions of the states. Federal funding tends to be directed to students of low-income families and those with learning disabilities, through ESEA I and the *Education Disabilities Act.* State and local funding patterns have regional and historic roots that produce a hodgepodge of formulas that defy brief summarization.

To illustrate the nature of the financial disparities and the politics of the cities, a recent legal challenge to failing schools in New York City brought a judicial ruling that the State of New York had failed to provide adequate funds to allow for the basic educational needs of children in the New York City schools. This was not a finding of inequity but of sheer inadequacy. The ruling called for the State of New York to increase its budgetary provision of public school financing to cover the costs of basic educational needs, a sum running into the billions of dollars. In an article, "Starving the Schools, It's time for the state and city to play fair," Bob Herbert writes:

State Supreme Court Justice Leland DeGrasse in a landmark ruling that is being appealed—has said, in effect, that you can't continue to subject New York City kids to a public school system that in many ways is like a nightmare out of Dickens. . . . He declared the state's method of financing the public schools illegal, saying it deprives city students of the "sound, basic education" guaranteed by the State Constitution. His ruling was unequivocal. It requires nothing less than an infusion of additional aid sufficient to achieve a profound improvement in the quality of education offered by the city's public schools.[1]

The Governor's budget in response to this ruling was to provide a far lesser sum than needed with a call for New York City to assume the burden of filling the gap of need, while the state pursued an appeal of the Judge's ruling. This sort of political and financial jousting between state and local authorities goes on across the nation, as political pressures are exerted to favor one side or the other. This often leads to formulas that attempt to define need and responsibility in a manner permitting political compromise but leaving the poorest school children in the lurch in terms of filling their needs. This pattern of education financing is one of the factors contributing to our horrible record of failing schools and classrooms across the nation, particularly in inner cities and minority-area schools.

In a like manner, having followed a practice of appeals and downright stonewalling, the state of New Jersey's new governor, James McGreevey, has reversed course. He announced the state would accede to the New Jersey Supreme Court's ruling that the state must equalize education funding among its school districts. The governor's decision came 22 years after the lawsuit was filed. In an editorial on this matter, *The New York Times* noted that the New Jersey decision would probably be as far-reaching in its effects on public education as *Brown v. Board of Education*. The editorial also noted "nearly 20 states have been jolted by court decisions ordering them to provide poor and minority students with equal access to quality schools."[2]

Unlike elementary and secondary education, higher education receives substantial federal funding, primarily through massive student aid programs, which directly aid students in need of grants, loans, work-study and other forms of assistance to pay for college. In effect, the federal programs provide financial access to postsecondary education to students from all income levels. Although these successful programs have opened the doors of higher education by assisting students financially who would not have otherwise be able to attend college, the irony of this federal contribution is to make higher education affordable for students who often are not prepared adequately by their secondary schools and who will, by and large, not remain in college.

GOVERNANCE PROBLEMS

As with funding for education, the politics of education is shifting toward the federal level. Education was the top domestic priority of both the Democratic and Republican parties until the terrorist attacks of September 11, 2001, which preempted all domestic issues for a period of time. Subsequently, however, the Bush Administration reached agreement with the Kennedy-led Democrats in the Congress to achieve education reform. One issue that has dominated the interest of both parties is how to make the schools work for the poor and minority students in the inner cities of the nation. The overwhelming evidence that African-American and Latino children are falling way behind in test scores and dropping out of the schools in much larger numbers than their white counterparts creates a discriminatory challenge to the predominantly white school establishment. Since schooling assures entry to careers, the economic reality is that minority populations will continue to fall behind in professional advancement and economic progress. Such racial disparity in opportunity and achievement is political dynamite, which can lead to social struggle for equality and political struggle for control and eventually a desire to legislate radical changes in the educational system. Politicians have been vying for solutions that will give them an advantage in solving the riddle of failing schools, but it has been an illusive chase for working answers. In the latest round of legislation, the main strategy is to achieve educational accountability through massive standardized testing in grades 3 through 8 in reading and mathematics with specified consequences to occur if the test scores do not improve. This new legislation also makes significant provisions for improving teacher preparation.

With regard to governance outside the political arena, public education is administered through a tangled web of bureaucratic structures, including the U.S. Department of Education, state departments of education, and local school systems, which vary in composition depending on geographic and historic factors. Boards of education representing the public are a common part of the system at state and local levels, and they are being bombarded with interest groups who are struggling for control of the education colossus. For example, in California, bilingual education has divided Hispanic and Anglo advocates over the school curriculum. In Virginia and other states, standards of performance and evaluation create tension between state and local authorities over the control of schools.

Higher education, on the other hand, has a different structure, which reflects the independence of colleges and universities and their tradition of reaching beyond political boundaries for their student bodies. The fact that higher education institutions compete nationally for their students makes the federal program for student aid the principal factor in influencing policies of access and continuation to higher education for all citizens. The politics of supporting and advocating for student access to higher education is now a major event that influences the life of our institutions of higher learning. The continuing struggle for equal educational opportunity by minority populations and low-income families is being translated into a major thrust for improvement in the system itself and for a massive advance in student aid programs to assure equal access to colleges.

Among all the components of governing the schools and colleges, from the Congress down to local school boards and boards of trustees, the factor that stands out in terms of influence and future significance is the expanded federal role. Only fifty years ago, the federal government was hardly a player at all in the education scene. The watchword in Congress, as well as among the states, was to keep the "feds" out of the schools and colleges, and certainly to avoid infringement on curriculum or programs by any federal body. To underscore this position, the then Office of Education was a minor agency within the huge Department of Health, Education and Welfare, and was often subject to heavy-handed supervision from the Secretary of that Department.

Today the Department of Education is a major funding source for all of postsecondary education with its massive student aid programs, which guarantee at least some college funding for all students. Additionally, the federal department plays an increasing role in both the funding and supervision of the public elementary and secondary school system, with major emphasis on equalizing the performance of the system for those who are disabled and disadvantaged.

Despite resistance at both the state and local levels, this invigorated federal presence is being broadly demonstrated in support for those who would otherwise be left out of education and in new standards of performance designed to infuse accountability measures throughout the system.

The federal financial contribution is still comparatively minimal at the elementary and secondary levels (about 10 percent, according to *The New York Times*), but it is likely to grow as the states and local jurisdictions find their financial resources eroding.[3]

If the federal government is the brash new kid on the block in the education community, the state departments of education are the established residents. And they have not been enamored of the "strings" tied to the federal dollars in terms of their requirements and guidelines. Traditionally, the states through these departments have overseen teaching and certification requirements; set standards for buildings, textbooks, testing, etc.; distributed state funds in accordance with the formulas developed by their respective legislatures; and provided other types of assistance to the school districts within their jurisdiction. In most instances, state departments are bureaucracies. They do not engage in the "hands on" administration of the schools, and hence they tend to be somewhat removed from the usual fray that the local school districts experience. In addition, state departments have little direct contact with teachers and students. In those states with big cities, like New York and Illinois, the state departments of education have had little control over their big city school systems. An exception is Pennsylvania where a private corporation, Edison Corp., is taking over portions of the city of Philadelphia's school system. In recent years, as the tax base of the cities has eroded, the conflicts between the state and local levels have escalated.

The majorities in the state legislatures often view their big cities as the enemy. Nowhere has this been truer than in New York. New York State alone has more than 53 funding formulas, which have been largely designed by legislators from the suburbs or districts outside of New York City. Together, such formulas combine to shortchange the public schools of the City of New York. Parents in several of the inner city areas have filed lawsuits against the state, and the chancellor of the New York City Schools is supporting them. The mayor of New York says he can't find the money to rescue the schools. A judge has already ruled that the education being provided in the city is inadequate and has told the state to pay up. The governor is appealing the decision. The city and state are stalemated, but the children of the city system continue to suffer. This situation is not unique; other cities are in the same fix.

Traditionally, administrative and programmatic decision-making and solutions have been the province of local school boards and their superintendents. All too often, these solutions have clearly involved making a single change. For example, it was thought that Computer Assisted Instruction (CAI) would allow everybody to proceed at his or her own pace. This situation has been going on for decades. The real question is: can the current structure of boards, school superintendents, and school officials really solve the problems facing beleaguered school systems and colleges? The answer is probably no.

We illustrate this answer by specifics. One very clever technique employed by boards to mollify the public, and to stay in power as well, can be seen in the selection of superintendents and university presidents. These techniques can be translated into mathematical-like formulas that go like this:

Formula 1: Hire a school superintendent or (less often, a university president) → shower the person with praise → community feels at ease for a while → school superintendent (university president) does a few highly noticeable things that don't make a difference or do make a mess → the person comes under attack by the board members, students, faculty, community leaders and/or politicians, the board engages in political posturing, etc. → the superintendent (president) is either fired or resigns → the collective community is uneasy → the board re-enters as the savior → the board hires a new superintendent (university president).

Formula 2: Repeat the cycle every two or three years, community feels at ease for a while → the board stays in power → the problems worsen every time.

Formula 3: (only to be used when Formula 2 doesn't pacify the community for long enough periods of time) Force City Hall or the legislature to appoint a new board → practice "omerta"—a Mafia term meaning to engage in collective silence and cover-up → then repeat Formula 2.

Let us show the formulas in action. When the finances of the District of Columbia were in chaos, and the school system was in well-publicized disarray, the U.S. Congress appointed a control authority to take over the finances of the District of Columbia. What was called the Control Board, in turn, abolished the elected school board and appointed a new board. The new school board appointed General Julius Becton, a friend of the Control Board chairman, to be the new superintendent. He was praised by the Control Board, the local politicians and many others involved with the process. The new school board calmed the fears of the community for a while. Superintendent Becton quit after 17 months, "saying he was worn down." The reaction of the Control Board members, as could be predicted, was one of disbelief. For example, one Control Board member, who was responsible for education matters and was the former acting president of Howard University, Dr. Joyce Ladner, stated, "It's all gone awry." Then the board had to fix this problem again.

The Control Board, after an extensive search, selected Arlene Ackerman as the next superintendent of the District of Columbia Public Schools. Ladner described Ackerman as a reformer and the one who would write the "final chapter" on D.C. schools. In her speech, "Reaching Higher: On the Road to Exemplary Achievement," she prepared a report card in which she gave a rating of D to F to a list of approximately 22 items.[4] Can anyone believe that she would be able to take a school system from a rating of D-F to "exemplary"? We question the intentions of these officials in using such "pie-in-the-sky" words. After less than two years Ackerman resigned, in the middle of 2000. Her main reason for leaving was her frustration over the board's failure to institute changes fast enough. Control Board chairman, Dr. Brimmer said, "[E]fforts to overhaul the school system have not turned out well though . . . Ackerman was making progress." However, another Control Board member, Dr. Cooper, countered, "They had all the power, but they didn't have the chutzpah to do it. . . . They created this mess."

After this debacle, the new school board hired another new superintendent, Paul L. Vance, for the District Public Schools in July of 2000. After seven months in the office in a school system where 40 percent of students drop out during their high school years, Vance reported that

> [He] is developing what he says will be a model procurement operation, and a new transportation administrator is working to revamp bus service for special education students. On a day-to-day basis, there are only modest signs of improvement in those areas, with some employees still receiving incorrect paychecks, students arriving at school late and purchasing orders delayed [a persistent problem for decades].[5]

Mr. Vance immediately confronted an entrenched bureaucracy, including the teachers' union, which has seen superintendents come and go like planes buzzing in and out of Reagan National Airport. Without sweeping powers to hire, fire, transfer, outsource and substitute, a newcomer soon falls prey to "those who know." Mr. Vance was hired primarily to improve the academics of a failing school system. Shouldn't he have been looking at his teaching staff, the demography of his student population, and ways to eliminate the layers between him and the frontline administrators—the principals? Instead, his major focus has been on improving the schools' procurement and transportation systems. Nothing like taking the scenic route to improving academic programs.

Now the chairman of the new board, Ms. Peggy Cooper Cafritz, has weighed in with a pronouncement that "about half of our high school teachers are not really masters of the content they teach."[6] Her remarks were half buried in the rush to announce a new teacher recruitment program that would attempt to attract content-qualified professionals and deal with their teacher certification later—perhaps even paying their attendant tuition bills.

Following up, an analyst for *The Washington Post*, Colbert King, prefaced his report on the D.C. Schools with the following comment:[7] "The District has seen a succession of superintendents, school board members and civic leaders who have regarded it as their bounden duty to serve as cheerleaders and apologists for a broken system of public education." Noting that it was safe to discuss only certain topics in public, such as "our nerdy mayor, Republicans in Congress and the folks who live in the suburbs," he pointed out that Cafritz had broken the longstanding code of silence in the District. This code is something we clearly understand, having worked for more than 25 years in the District. A phrase typical of the code is "It's a mess, but it's our mess—and stay out of it." King reported an interview with Cafritz in which she provided the background and the backup for her assertion. But the most devastating part of the analysis was the following comment:

> If they (Vance and Cafritz) have a plan to address their concerns about bad teachers, their distress over principals who can't manage their schools or properly evaluate their instructors, or what to do about children who arrive at school unprepared to learn, I missed it. But hand this to them: They really know how to do a number on everybody else.

One of the institutions that really has had a number done on it by the D.C. Schools' underprepared students and City Hall's dumping ground practices for tired politicians and cronies is the University of the District of Columbia. Consolidated from three separate institutions in the late 1970s, UDC started out with high hopes and a large enrollment. Because of its charter to provide affordable education to residents of the District of Columbia as the city's only public institution of higher education, UDC was required to focus its main effort on these District residents. As might be expected, the main feeder system to the university is the D.C. Schools, recently characterized as "a broken system of public education" by King. In a similar vein, Cafritz "chalked up the current dismal condition of D.C. public education to 'a total and complete disintegration of a system that has happened over the last 30 years.'"

And the graduates of this school system have come to the university—those who could not afford to go elsewhere or those who had been out of high school for a while, thinking they were prepared for college-level work. A shock was waiting for them. Most found that they were nowhere near the reading, writing, and mathematics levels required for college-level work. The university faculty, taking its mission seriously, suddenly found itself in the business of trying to bring these graduates up to college level work. Under the euphemistic term of developmental education, courses in English, reading and mathematics were implemented, and the number of sections required in these areas rose astronomically, tying up around 80 percent of the university's resources.

Some years later, with regard to the university, Cafritz stated, "90 percent of UDC's . . . population comes from the D.C. public school system and 90 percent of those are in remedial education." As a result, the university's mission was seriously eroded as it tried to serve its constituency. The total enrollment dropped from a high of 14,000 students to approximately 5000, and the number of departments was reduced from a high of 52 to the current 16. The faculty has been seriously pared, and the number of upper level courses seriously reduced. The university's budget has been cut by almost 50 percent during the past several years. The university has changed presidents and provosts every two or three years on average.

The whole public education system of the District of Columbia from kindergarten to the master's level is in dire straits. UDC is continually looking for a new president and has just appointed a new one, and its provosts have been repeatedly fired. Mr. Vance may or may not remain. Other public education systems in urban areas are facing similar situations, but they are not situated in the capital of the most powerful nation in the world.

A similar situation is currently playing itself out in Prince Georges County in Maryland where the current school superintendent, Iris Metts, was fired by the school board and then reinstated by the courts and the state. In the meantime, the school system is in turmoil over this conflict, and student learning is suffering.

Hiring one person at the top does not change a school system, an axiom that is aptly illustrated by William Raspberry, an analyst for *The Washington Post*. He stated:

[The assumption is] that the people, who run and staff our low-performing public schools, could do a much better job if they wanted to. So why do so many inner city and rural schools fail? The first thing about the question is how few superintendents and other school officials seem to be asking it. Instead, they point out a dozen things—smaller classes, spiffier buildings, newer computers—that are lacking, leading one to conclude that supplying these things will produce success. It seldom happens. Why does it happen so seldom?[8]

At the heart of the answer to this question is the equating of educational supports with the learning process itself. Moreover, the educational supports are much easier to implement in the short term than improvements in the learning process, which are long term. The ultimate consequence of this is a short tenure for most school superintendents in troubled school districts.

THE FAMILY

As we noted earlier, the schools have always commanded most of a child's prime time during the critical years of development. When women were home while their children were away in school, they were busy with many household-management non-paying activities. They also engaged in other activities outside of the home, including participation in the schools, as well as in remunerated tasks. When a child is in school, the caregiving parent does not necessarily have to be at home. For this reason alone, it seems simplistic and inaccurate to criticize parents who choose to work or who find it necessary to work, mainly during school hours or even slightly longer. In today's society, the one-income family is becoming increasingly rare. The much-vaunted nuclear family of working father, stay-at-home mother and two or so children now comprises less than 18 percent of the families in the United States. Instead, a combination of economic and civil rights developments has now resulted in single-parent families, extended families, blended and same-sex families in addition to the nuclear family. The wails in society about the breakdown of the family fail to take into account the many forms that family can take in order to make an economic and socially cohesive go of it, and they ignore changes in child-rearing practices that have made families much less authoritarian and much more egalitarian in their internal social structure. Whether we like all these forms and changes or not, they are part of contemporary society, and as with technological advances, they are not going away. Also, let us keep in mind that the opportunities for and the roles of women will expand, and the number of working women will increase; this change is irreversible and therefore must be taken into account for all school planning, academic offerings, and educational programming. Certainly, after school programs are one answer, and these can range from academic to recreational. For many children, having a quiet place to study, read, receive a little tutoring, engage in a hobby or project, or just relax and watch a movie or listen to music with friends would be a welcome addition in their lives. Teachers, being given extra money, could supervise such activities in after-school programs. In effect, the schools must pick up where the family does not or cannot. As a frontline agency with the necessary equipment and space, the schools must engage in such life-saving roles.

TECHNOLOGY, COMPUTERS AND THE INTERNET

Technology, computers and their application software (word processing, spreadsheet, databases and presentation) and the Internet are here to stay. Their various roles in society undoubtedly will expand. And the humble course, Typing, has suddenly become elevated to the gateway course for using computers and the Internet under the upscaled title, Keyboarding. Despite this new status, many potential users and actual users cannot comfortably employ the computer, including the Internet, effectively because they do not know keyboarding. Complicating the problem still further is the view of those who contend that the Internet is having a negative impact on children's learning and schools. One author who argues this case is Diane Ravitch, who comments "Large social, economic, and technological changes have undermined the family, made people more mobile, and communities less stable, and turned adolescents into consumers whose dollars are ardently pursued by savvy advertisers."[9]

The statements may or may not be true, but let's face it: the Internet and other high-tech inventions cannot be stopped; they are not going away. The real problem is not with the Internet; rather the real problem is with the schools and teachers who do not comprehend its enormous potential for teaching and learning. The Internet is a new approach to obtaining information quickly; adolescents are naturally attracted to new things. One way to view the Internet is like a nifty rummage sale—without price tags, in which one can browse in the convenience of one's home. As with all rummage sales, there are treasures and trash. Young people can be taught to differentiate between them.

Teachers must recognize the Internet's value, its continuing presence, and its allure for young people. Even more importantly, teachers must be taught

CHAPTER 3

to use the Internet and computers. Then, after the teachers learn to use the technology, they need to teach their students how to use it on a selective basis. However, this kind of use can happen only if the teachers are fully conversant with the Internet and understand its potential for student learning. Any teacher who is not comfortable using the Internet is likely to view it in a negative light and will be unable to use it for research, information, and other academic activities that could benefit students.

Placed in a historical perspective, technology has proven to be a double-edged sword for educational purposes. On the one hand, it has been hailed as a panacea for self-paced student learning, using CAI (Computer Aided Instruction), a strategy that only seems to work with the very able and self-confident student. On the other hand, it has been condemned as preventing students from learning. For example, the hand calculator has been blamed by both parents and teachers for youngsters not learning basic math. Instead of blaming the calculators and computers—and the latest entry, the Internet—for kids not learning, we should find strategies that incorporate new technology in an effective way that can enhance learning and teaching. What has also been interesting about so-called technological solutions to student learning is that the teacher is relegated to the background, serving supposedly in a consultative role.

Now back to the calculator for a moment: the real problem here is that basic math has not been adequately taught (e.g., the multiplication tables, simple addition and subtraction, fractions and ratios) before using the calculator. For example, one math teacher in her Algebra I class ". . . wrote equations with a jumble of x's, y's and square root signs on the overhead projector. She promised to demystify the quadratic formula. 'My head hurts,' said one student, using a calculator to figure out what $-4 + 11$ equals."[10] And she is trying to teach this kid algebra!

ADOLESCENCE, HEDONISM AND THE CULTURE

Our culture extols physical beauty and athletic prowess, and assorted forms of instant gratification, such as alcohol consumption, making big money, and the material good things of life. Also extolled are individual independence and achievement. In a sort of bizarre echo of their usage by the adults in society, adolescents have adopted some of these for their own purposes: alcohol in the form of binge drinking parties, individual independence in the form of freedom of movement as a result of having access to cars, and extremely

30

innovative uses of the cell phone to cover their absences from home for long periods of time and facilitate their communication with one another in the maintenance of the out-of-school search for parties and other pleasures. This last point is clearly documented by Patrick Welsh,[11] an English teacher at a local public high school and an occasional commentator on the teen scene for *The Washington Post*. In an article entitled, "The Party Line," he makes it clear that the students involved in the party network, including his own daughter, are not in any way to be considered as troublemakers or potential dropouts. Quite the contrary, some are honor students, all are potentially college bound, all come from "good" homes. What has evolved is a further variant of adolescent subculture.

What's happened? Why are students doing this? Welch points out that they see the drinking at home (although not binge drinking). The cars are available, and the cell phones are around the house, too. Teenagers find attempts to enforce the drinking age to be ridiculous. Welch quotes one senior as saying

> [T]he drinking laws are a joke. We can go into battle and kill someone, vote and drive a car by the time we're 18, but we can't have a drink until we are 21. That gives kids a lot to rebel against and leads to excess . . . [Another senior noted] that half the fun of drinking is going out and buying the booze, because it's forbidden.

However, Welch pointed out that the students have developed some ground rules of their own. For example, if a girl becomes "totally drunk," her friends, both female and male, step in "and see that she gets home safely." Also, those who are driving others generally drink less. But is it right to throw the entire burden basically upon the young people?

As with other features of our society, this party culture and its "forbidden fruit" of alcohol and drugs are not going away any time soon. Several things stand out to us about this situation. First, these are really young adults. Second, running through this article are indicators of a sense of personal responsibility and, perhaps even more importantly, of possible solutions suggested by students themselves, e.g., raising the driving age, so that kids don't have access to cars and must rely on parents or other adults, as well as involving schools in dealing with the "party culture."

What can be done about this situation? Why not have the students suggest solutions and then permit them to organize themselves to carry out the proposals? During the school day or at evening sessions, why not have teachers and other adults, including parents, listen to and discuss the teen world with all its pressures, distractions, and activities with these young adults? Let them decide on the activities; set the ground rules, including adult intervention; be responsible for carrying them out; and handle the violators. And why not carry out these activities on school property? We wonder just how much of the so-called party culture is an escape from the pressures that are being placed upon these young adults to perform and succeed. Also, it may fall into the time-honored human trait of experimenting with the forbidden. Adam and Eve did the big apple; these students are doing alcohol and other drugs. But the principle is the same. These young adults are perfectly capable of working out constructive solutions.

Two instances of student self-governance, in which the authors participated, occurred at the University of the District of Columbia. In one case, the authors, as a function of a grant from the U.S. Department of Education, established a general-purpose computer laboratory, the "Pentium III Lab", for students, which was to be managed by the students as well. There were concerns that small items, like the staplers, pens, pencils, paper clips, computer speakers, laser printing paper, etc., would be taken away by the students as vandalism. To illustrate our point, in anticipation of our concerns regarding pilferage, we purchased 12 staplers. All office supplies, including the staplers, were placed in the lab for student use on the opening day of the lab. We kept on saying to ourselves that one of these days small items will be stolen from the lab. However, to the surprise of everyone, not a single item was removed, and after three years, the students were still using the original stapler. Everyone involved was proved wrong about the behavior of students.

In another instance, the authors were involved in the training of high school students from Anacostia High School, Washington, D.C., to study the impact of technology (computer productivity software) on the academic performance of minority and poor students when they were in eleventh and twelfth grades. Once again, we were warned about the behavior of these students in terms of vandalizing a facility. The training program was carried out at the Scientific Parallel Processing Applied Research Center (SPPARC), UDC, for approximately six years. The training was conducted once a week for 12 weeks per semester. The "lab manager" was usually a student of UDC who had graduated from the District's high school system. To our surprise, we did not have one incidence of vandalism of any kind. This was because we treated these students like the young adults they were.

VIOLENCE AND THE EDUCATION PSYCHE

Not so long ago the word "columbine" conjured up a beautiful spring blooming flower. For Colorado, it is special—the blue columbine is the state flower. But recent events have changed all that: the word now evokes thoughts of student violence because of the shootings at Columbine High School in Littleton, Colorado, and other instances that have occurred since then. For example, one article[12] in *The New York Times* itemized 21 instances of school violence or threats of violence in various states since Columbine. In every instance, police action and disruption of the school day were involved.

Now school systems are developing elaborate procedures for guarding against violence—often without thinking through the consequences of these so-called protective procedures. For example, the concept of zero-tolerance eliminates any kind of room or leeway for spoofing, banter or lightly intended commentary that carries words like kill or murder. It may even pose a challenge to an angry or disturbed student to gain attention through beating the system. Metal detectors, book bag searches or bans, procedures and code words for classroom lock-downs are real tension builders, no matter how well the reasons for their use are understood by all concerned. Such actions can only have a negative effect on the classroom. The landscape of teaching and learning has been altered and with it student and teacher relationships. "The age of anxiety" can be said to characterize a new venue: the schools.

And the American public is now being forced to look at a phenomenon that has always been a part of the education system but has never before had the klieg lights of the media trained on it. What is this phenomenon? It is a witch's brew of unchecked bullies, isolated victims, myopic cliques, and too many "look-the-other-way" adults. When easy access to dangerous weapons is added to the brew, the potential for a disastrous explosion increases.

Why do certain students feel so isolated? Do cliques form only for mutual self-protection and self-reinforcement? Why is adolescent student dress so uniformly the same? Because of a fear of being different, of being singled out from the herd, of being unloved, of being abandoned. Above all, why do school officials often tacitly allow situations involving scapegoating and bullying to happen through their not being present, physically or psychologically?

Let's look at the principal players here. Bullies are behaviorally aberrant individuals. Their size, their strength, their quick tempers or their skill at some punishing behavior makes them feared—particularly by individuals who are no physical match for them. But make no mistake about it: bullies are not within the parameters of normal human beings. They are basically fragile personalities. They seek attention. When they don't receive it through more conventional avenues, they achieve it through hurting and torturing others; it's the main way they can sustain a sense of self-worth.

But both bullies and their victims are socially isolated from their more socially and academically successful peers. Bullies may be tolerated because of fear, but victims ironically are not. Victims suffer rejection, humiliation, and isolation in some public situations by others, usually popular students or members of recognized desirable cliques that the particular child or adolescent truly wants to be part of. Indeed, victims are often blamed for what happens to them because they make people around them feel uncomfortable, even guilty. When this situation is compounded by non-observant behaviors—deliberate, uncaring, or innocent—which in themselves are a form of self-imposed isolation, either from other students or from adults in the immediate environment, the stage is set for attention-getting, destructive behavior. The latter possibility is enhanced, of course, if the individual has ready access to a dangerous weapon. This behavior can take the form of overt actions against others—killing or hurting students and adults in the setting associated with the bullying. Or, the behavior can be turned onto the individual himself, even going as far as suicide.

For the bully, the consequences may be minimal or long-delayed, because the bully's victims do not go after the actual attacker directly, but usually find a surrogate of sorts. But sooner or later, bullies run into trouble; the need to hurt eventually backfires.

Then how do we deal with the problem of bullying? Based on our years of teaching experience, we contend that the answer lies in socialization. Bullies are only partially socialized. Victims usually are reasonably socialized, but their socialization takes the form of being over-sensitized to their peers and being very dependent upon what their peers think or they perceive their peers as thinking. Usually, some physical trait causes them to be perceived by their peers as being different. Group work and group accountability for academic performance really *do* work in a classroom. For example, one of us consistently used collaborative efforts in teaching research methods with students who normally would not have much to say to one another because of their diversity in terms of age, ethnic membership, family status, sexual orientation, etc. They turned out to have a great deal to say to and do for one another, when faced with a common task. In the end, these students turned in far more insightful and comprehensive research projects than did students working alone, and they came to have a genuine appreciation of each other's talents and contributions. There is nothing God-given about doing one's homework assignment in mathematics or statistics or English by oneself; why not assign the problems collaboratively? The icky-looking nerd who sits off to one side and likes doing extra problems in mathematics might just turn out to be a terrific mentor for students who could use a little help. The bully may need help in reading or math; this person often does. Rarely is a bully a good student. Find a way to put this individual into a situation where help can be given—maybe by peers—without a putdown and where he or she can make a contribution.

What is even more devastating is ignoring instances of bullying as if they did not occur or treating them as a part of normal behavior. Sheer observation is important. Bullies don't like being observed by someone "in authority." Officials need to be informed; bullies need to be dealt with. Set them a task that can constructively use their strength or whatever may be their skill. Find ways of removing them from situations where they can be bullies. Enlist student leaders to work with school officials in developing civility codes for school and grounds activities and in being watchful for bullying behavior and (anonymously) reporting it. Without publicly targeting particular students as either bullies or victims, regular scheduled meetings among teachers and other school officials should be encouraged to find ways to improve the socialization process in and out of the educational environment. Punishment is only a short-term answer; suppressed behavior does not go away. Socialization is the long-term answer; positive behavior changes in this area are good for life.

As a final note here, we can again recollect John Donne's observation: "No man is an island/every man is part of the main . . . ." Instead, both in the classroom and with homework assignments, we typically tend to treat every student as being an island far apart from one another—*and* the main. Since the world basically operates in groups—civilization never would have developed without them—why are teachers and other school officials flying in the face of the successful practices proven over centuries?

NOTES

1. Herbert, B. (2001, January 22). Starving the Schools, It's Time for the State and City to Play Fair. *The New York Times,* p. A23.

2. Herbert (2002, February 9). A Truce in New Jersey's School War. *The New York Times.* Editorial, p. A26.

3. Halstead, T. (2002, January 8). Rich School, Poor School. *The New York Times,* p. A23.

4. http://www.k12.dc.us/dcps/what's_new/speeches/Ackerman_speech.html

5. Blum, J. (2001, February 18). At Midterm, D.C. Superintendent Gets Mixed Review. *The Washington Post.* p. C4.

6. Blum, J. (2001, February 23). Half of District Teachers Weak, Board Chief Says. *The Washington Post,* p. B3.

7. King, C. I. (2001, February 24). A Public Spanking for D.C. Schools. *The Washington Post,* p. A23.

8. Raspberry, W. (2000, May 12). They Never Learn. *The Washington Post,* p. A47.

9. Ravitch, D. (2000). *Left Back.* New York: Simon & Schuster, p. 456.

10. Schulte, B. (2000, May 9). Montgomery [County] Tries to Solve Math Problem: Algebra Is a Concern, Especially for Minorities. *The Washington Post.* p. B1.

11. Welch, P. (2001, March 4). The Party Line. *The Washington Post,* p. B1.

12. Zernike, K. (2001, March 24). After Shootings, Schools Struggle to Find Best Response to Threats. *The New York Times,* p. A1.

4

TODAY'S CLASSROOM

Spiffy buildings, new equipment and materials, updated curricula, adequate procurement practices and personnel management are only in supporting roles to the main actors in the drama: the teacher and the students. The classroom is where the mission assigned to the public schools by our society either succeeds or fails. This mission is played out over time, in successive classrooms, with individual teachers working with the students who come to them. And the evidence is steadily accruing that in too many of these classrooms, the educative process is simply not working with too many students. When this process doesn't work in the classrooms, then the schools are defaulting on their mission not only to society as a whole, but also to those individuals who come to it. The students who drop out and don't return deprive us of their talents and will also cost us more because of their inadequate preparation to function effectively in society. Ultimately, everybody loses when we throw children away.

We have become convinced that few people both inside and outside of the classroom have any real conception of the enormous complexity involved in teaching. When the teaching situation involves diverse students with widely varying levels of preparation, the difficulty of teaching effectively increases exponentially. For example, a ninth grade student sitting in an English class may be reading at the fourth grade level and writing at the third. Another student in a ninth grade algebra class cannot add or subtract double digit numbers that require "carrying" or "borrowing." These students are not at all uncommon. Sitting in these same classes are probably children of recent immigrants who cannot read or write English. And the teachers are expected to teach all of them. In this chapter, we take a look at some of these problems.

POPULATION DIVERSITY—SOME NEW LOOKS FOR THE TWENTY-FIRST CENTURY

Diversity means differences from the "mainstream," as perceived by the established residents/citizens of a country, and these differences typically include language, cultural values, economic status, and the most obvious one of all, dress and cosmetic appearance. Unfortunately, these differences have become overly magnified as an aftermath of the September 11, 2001 terrorist attacks on New York City and Washington, D.C., in every public venue, and the schools have been no exception.

Yet, America is a nation of immigrants, and likely to stay that way. All along, when large numbers of immigrants have entered the country, diversity also has come with them. Nowhere has this been truer than in the twentieth century. In its first decade, 1901–1910, the majority of legal immigrants came from Europe (8,056,040). Next came Asia with 323,549, followed by Mexico with 49,642 and a scant 25,472 from Central and South America combined. Africa had the least with 7,368. Throughout the century, the numbers ebbed and flowed.

But a terrific shift in the origins of immigrants has occurred in the last decade of the twentieth century. In 1998, the most recent year for which the *Immigration and Naturalization Service Yearbook*[1] reports figures, legal immigrants from Europe had dwindled to approximately 1,152,000. Asia was out in front with 2,346,000, trailed only slightly by Mexico with 1,931,000 (excluding the 3,000,000 illegal immigrants already in the country). The legal figure for Mexico alone is more than the rest of Latin America combined, which were slightly over 1,000,000. When the Hispanic groups are combined, and the "illegals" from Mexico are included, the numbers from Latin countries total 6,000,000. Africa has weighed in with only 280,000, and Oceania is negligible. Contributing to these large variations in the numbers have been U.S. immigration policies (never impartial) during each of the time periods, as well as changing social conditions in both the countries of origin and the United States.

One characteristic of the latest influx of immigrants is that they have tended to settle in only a limited number of areas, specifically, New York City and its near suburbs, New Jersey, Florida, Texas, Illinois—usually Chicago, and southern California. Other areas, like the ring of suburbs around Washington, D.C., are feeling substantial impacts as well. Demographic maps based on the results of the 2000 census clearly show the most heavily impacted areas. The tendency of the newcomers voluntarily to cluster in ethnic and economic enclaves in order to feel more comfortable in their new land leads to another form of *de facto* segregation. Both the sheer numbers of immigrants and their clustering patterns pose tremendous challenges to the existing services and resources of those jurisdictions in which they have settled. One of these challenges is educating the children of these immigrants, a challenge that must be immediately fielded by the public education system at every level of the enterprise. Only the well-to-do and the educated professionals coming into the country show a scatter pattern in where they live, because they have choices and they speak English. Thus, diversity always carries an initial challenge for *both* the newcomers and those who are already here.

Clearly recognizing that education is the key to realizing the American dream, the demand of most of the immigrants becomes, "Teach us, too. We want in." But to access this educational opportunity, the newcomers must learn the language in which it is available: English. And they must learn it as rapidly as possible; an ESL course for an hour or two a day does not bring a secondary student up to the level of fluency needed for the content subjects of English, mathematics, science, social studies, etc. Most of the school systems are trying hard to accomplish this task, but the numbers and variety of immigrant languages make the task a daunting one. In one close-in suburban school system of Washington, D.C., approximately 128 languages are being spoken, and polylingual assistance is simply not available. So the children struggle.

Relatives of one of the authors have been in the ESL program of the Fairfax County Public Schools for over two years, and both youngsters are still scrambling to bring their English up to the needed proficiency levels to perform well in their other high school courses. A five- to six-week total immersion program in English, the type used by the military and international organizations to train their key personnel, would eliminate this language problem and would have sent these new immigrants into class with the necessary fluency to be successful in their courses. Yet no special provision has been made at either the federal or state levels to address the needs of children and youth who either do not speak or read English or who have only a very limited capability in it. The local school districts are struggling with it. If we do not solve the problem, we jeopardize both their and our futures.

But language is not the only problem facing immigrant groups: culture and poverty are also major problems. For example, Hispanics, on their way to becoming the dominant minority group in the United States, generally accord a low priority to education. In a long article on this situation, *The New York Times* reported that "26 percent of Hispanic girls leave school without a diploma, compared with 13 percent of black girls and 6.9 percent of white girls." Hispanic boys had an even worse rate: 31 percent as "compared with 12.1 percent of black boys and 7.7 percent of white boys."[2] The dropout rate of Asians was never mentioned. Both culture and poverty enter into the picture very directly. Because of economic necessity, Hispanic teenagers are under pressure to contribute to the family either by finding jobs or by babysitting while adults work. From a cultural standpoint, grandparents pressure girls to become wives and mothers. While some of their teachers and mothers tell the girls they can have careers first and boyfriends second, many of their teachers expect them to drop out. Also, Hispanic families strive to maintain their native language, Spanish, which tends to slow the acquisition of English, necessary for achieving in school and the competitive U.S. workplace. Sex education for girls is rarely given, and pregnancy is acceptable in the early and middle teen years. The result is a confusing message—particularly for the girls, according to spokespersons in the Hispanic community.[3] When these families live in basically Spanish-speaking neighborhoods, the children become even further isolated from the mainstream.

Another minority group that has long struggled to climb out of poverty and negative stereotypes has been the African American population. While the group, as a whole, has made major gains in the latter half of the twentieth century in terms of education, employment, and political representation, largely resulting from the civil rights thrusts of the 1960s many African Americans have not gained parity with their white counterparts. Other immigrant and minority groups have arrived in this country, experienced initial oppression, gradually gained in status, and have been accepted. But for African Americans, the pattern has been different. Coming to this country largely against their will, impressed into slavery, then into second-class citizenship after the Civil War, and finally gaining legal parity a century later, this group is still struggling to gain full acceptance.

One place where parity has yet to be achieved is in educational preparation and achievement: African Americans, by and large, continue to lag behind their majority counterparts, particularly in the sciences. Many people have attempted to explain this phenomenon, and the explanations have comprised a dreary litany of "in vogue" causes: racial inferiority, social promotion, the black family, poverty, a value system that rewards "dumbing down," etc. One very recent explanation has come from John McWhorter,[4] an African

American linguist, who argues for a black self-imposed ideology composed of a "Cult of Victimology, Separatism, and Anti-intellectualism," an ideology that he states is condoned by whites. One net effect of all of these causes is an image of the African American student that is deficient in comparison with his white counterpart. The code word for this African American student has been "nonstandard," and it has been used as a justification for teachers to lower their expectations for these students and for not teaching them. While lowered expectations can be viewed as part of the problem, they are not the whole of it. A large part of the problem is that the teachers of these students are themselves often only marginally qualified in both content and pedagogy. Another part of the problem is pointed out by Raspberry when he notes, "[M]any teachers don't know as much as they should about teaching 'nonstandard children'—because their teachers' colleges didn't teach them about it. But that doesn't mean they're too dumb to do it."[5]

We also believe that teachers are not dumb, but when you don't know, you must be taught. This problem of finding and/or training teachers is not going to be solved until we recognize that the art of teaching is an enormously complex task for which substantive hands-on preparation is mandatory.

THE OTHER CIVIL RIGHT—READING

Reading really is a wondrous tool of empowerment, opening doors to everywhere and everything, but school systems have succeeded in making it into nothing but drudgery for children and teachers alike. As the requirements of the society go up, up, up in reading, writing and mathematics, the performance of the schools in preparing the next generation in these areas seems to be going down, down, down. The newspapers are full of the problems in teaching reading and mathematics, although writing is beginning to surface as a major area of difficulty. However, at the present time, the problems with reading can probably be declared the clear winner on the grounds of national and localized literacy reports, test scores and just sheer verbiage. Perhaps no other area of the education program has had so much written about it, and so little in the way of progress achieved in it, as the area of reading. Nowhere are the schools having more problems than in teaching their students how to read. And the problems are likely to escalate as the school systems—particularly those with inner-city schools—scramble to fill their classroom teaching vacancies with live bodies who themselves know how to read, but probably haven't a clue about how to teach someone who doesn't—let alone a full class of such "someone's."

What is there about the teaching of reading that has made it such a chamber of horrors for so many teachers and students? There is no simple answer. First off, the act of reading is a highly skilled visual-perceptual, motor, memory-laden, cognitive-language task requiring focused attention for specified time periods. And how's that for a brainteaser! Like a great sports performance, when reading is done well, it appears to be effortless, and many of us forget the process underlying the reading act. That many six-year-old children make progress learning how to do it is a miracle as is their earlier acquisition of heard and spoken language.

Second, the so-called experts in the field of reading cannot agree on what it takes to learn how to read, because they differ on what constitutes reading. Currently, the fad is for phonics even though it is just one particular set of the word analysis skills. Let us keep in mind that English is not really a phonetic language. For example, some letters are silent in spoken words as in "through," "heart," or "neigh," and a given vowel can take on different meanings in words that are pronounced the same way, as in "to," "two," and "too." In contrast to a vowel sounding the same in spoken words, the same vowel can take on different sounds in common words as in "tot," "to," "tow," "towel," "work," and "monkey." The most commonly used words in the English language are not phonetic, an example being those compiled in the *Dolch 220 Basic Sight Vocabulary List* by Edward Dolch, an early specialist in the field of reading.

Third, it is important we recognize that reading is not just another subject-matter content handed down to teachers to teach from in the form of books, rather it is a cognitive process consisting of perception and language that must be learned before reading can begin. The process includes: developing visual-motor coordination and attention span; observing nutrition intake; motivating students to make the effort to learn; teaching auditory and visual discrimination, phonetic analysis, and comprehension techniques; and emphasizing the importance of retention though practice and memorization. However, most elementary teachers treat reading as a subject-matter content, which it is not. The materials they are given for teaching reading also treat it as a special content, although the content used often is not relevant to the students. These well-known facts (coupled with the anxiety of school administrators about reading) have opened the door to "teacher proofing" reading textbooks by both their authors and publishers (formerly known as "cookbook" readers). All the teachers have to do is follow the recipes (or scripts) given in the teacher's manual—and presto the students learn to read (maybe). Teachers have no other choice than following such a script, because they rarely have taken courses in teaching reading, even at the elementary level.

Another major problem begins in the first grade. Rather than starting at the level where the children are in the reading readiness process, many teachers assume first graders are all ready to learn how to read. Not so. A few children may already be reading, some may be ready to begin where the teacher's manual says they should be, and others may be far below the levels of visual and auditory perception and length of attention span required. They lack the motivation to make the effort and have no experience of being read to by adults, of which both are required for effectively learning how to read.

The situation becomes more complicated with diverse populations in school systems where many beginning students may not be speakers of English when they enter first grade. The problem worsens when the content in the textbooks has no relevance to the students' environment. As a consequence, students who still are not beginning readers by the time they leave the first grade, are already in academic jeopardy. This problem worsens when teachers themselves are not adequately trained in reading.

Over time this problem of reading readiness is compounded because the teaching of the reading process as an end in itself is typically completed by the end of the third grade. This marks a point where many students may not have yet learned the process dimension of reading. By this time, however, reading begins to be used more as a means to an end: instruction in the content fields of science, mathematics, social studies and English, which commence in the fourth grade. If a child does not read adequately by this time, his chances of learning to do so are seriously reduced. Thus the fourth grade becomes the reading epiphany for many children. With each succeeding grade, the demand for reading increases, and the reading tasks become more complex. If children have been taught well at the beginning, their reading abilities will typically improve as a function of completing assignments and receiving feedback on them. If a child has not been taught well, or parents do not intervene to find help, or the school doesn't pick up on the default, or the child is not very determined, then children in this predicament inevitably will fall behind, even though seemingly progressing adequately from grade to grade. Beginning at the ninth grade, the demands again markedly increase in the various disciplines. There is increased freedom in student selection of courses and less and less opportunity for any "catch up" in the reading process. Another epiphany is reached for the inner-city or rural student who is a poor reader or virtual non-reader, and the choices for these students are very clear: to stay and struggle and probably fail or just to disappear.

Everyone knows that children who have been read to at home are good risks for learning to read. But the situation changes radically when children come from homes where reading is not important, the necessities of life are barely available, adults may or may not be present, daily living is chaotic, or the language spoken is different from that of the school. Children from these circumstances don't have examples before them that are filled with reading and show reading as an integral part of daily life. Reading hardly exists in their lives; they haven't really seen any need for it. So, with no real reason for learning, why would a child invest the energy to learn how to read? Add to the mix reading material that is silly, irrelevant or boring to boot, and the situation worsens. And what six- or seven-year-old child can truly grasp that his future really does depend on his learning to read right now when he is tired, malnourished, trying to survive a fragile home life, and/or dealing with the streets? If the child is a non-English-speaking immigrant, the English words on the printed page mean nothing to him, except, perhaps, failure, embarrassment, and a sense of isolation. Again, the miracle of learning to read does occur for some of these children, but for too many, it does not.

As the continuing problems in teaching children to read clearly demonstrate, no canned reading program will work for every child. A teacher must recognize when the reading program is failing and must realize that adjustments need to be made. A teacher trained in reading who can make the necessary adjustments to their students' needs and interests just might make a difference. Let us cite an example.

In a previous incarnation, one of us, having been both trained and active in the field of reading, served for a time as the director of a reading clinic, and among other things designed a reading program for first grade Latino children, who exhibited all of the characteristics described above. Working with two volunteer teachers and writing original materials that dealt with the self concept and handling such emotions as fear, anger and joy, a team of three brought these children into fluency in spoken and written English. At the end of the first grade, the children had an average third grade reading level in English according to the reading section of the *Metropolitan Achievement Test: Primary Level*. Many of the word analysis skills had been taught, and the comprehension skills of main idea and supporting details, cause and effect, time and logical sequences, and analogy had all been worked on. Each class had a huge book, four feet tall and six feet across when opened, bound in red corduroy and mounted on a specially built easel in which they kept their "stories" with all the authors' names attached.

Groups of students could, in effect, "sit" in their book to read and discuss. For these children—for a little while at least, school and reading combined to be a magical thing.

This example dealt with the first grade. The situation becomes increasingly more complicated as we climb the ladder of grades. Secondary teachers focus on content—not on teaching the reading process in their disciplines— even though they may have some training in teaching methodology. But when we arrive at the postsecondary level, professors are not trained in any teaching methodology at all. The terminal degree in the particular discipline is all that is required in the college classroom. And nobody is specifically trained in the reading requirements for a given discipline. Everyone assumes students are proficient readers. Assignments are made, and if the students cannot handle them at all, they will drop out, because education at this level is not mandatory.

Let us give another example at the post-secondary level. Recently, one of us was teaching "Orientation to Higher Education," a first-semester-freshman required course at UDC and often assigned to faculty "for experience with our new students." In this instance, the task involved locating and then reading aloud a short section from the textbook in answer to a question. The first student called upon could not pronounce the three-syllable word, "civilize." After talking with her, it became apparent she had not a clue as to how to begin to analyze the word, and she had labored so hard to pronounce the words in the section that she had lost all its overall meaning. A check with the other students using other words revealed that of the 20 students in the class, 14 did not know how to divide a word into syllables, knew only a few phonetic rules, and could not derive some sense of the meaning from the surrounding context, which might have helped them recognize particular words. In short, they lacked the word analysis skills that characterize the second and third grade levels of reading instruction. And what is worse, these students don't even know that they don't know how to read at the elementary level, let alone the college level. Yet they had high school degrees and passing grades. While all but one of the students in this particular class had been assigned to "developmental courses" in both English and mathematics, it was apparent that their reading skills were far below the level of even these courses.

Such students are not unique in either the University of the District of Columbia or the city of Washington itself. Reports of two groups in the District, State Education Agency for Adult Education at UDC and the Washington Literacy Council, both stated that "62 percent of city residents are in the [two] lowest levels of reading proficiency . . . [giving] the District the distinction of having the lowest level literacy proficiency in the nation."[6] King also cited a separate federal study that estimated that "37 percent of the District's adults have Level 1 literacy skills." At this level, individuals may be able to sign their names or read an expiration date on their driver's licenses, but they cannot handle maps, "fill out an application for a Social Security card, read prescription and food labels, read a story to a child."[7] The two earlier reports suggest that about 25 percent of District residents are at Level 2, unable to: write a business letter or read a bus schedule or newspaper article. This 62 percent translates to 130,000 adults along with a high school dropout rate of 40 percent. Of course, the consequences for people with these literacy problems are horrific in terms of job opportunities, participation in community life, child rearing, etc.

If Washington is an extreme—and appalling—example, as the nation's capital, it is not alone. Other cities and rural areas have similar problems. The U.S. Department of Education estimates that at least 25 percent of the population reads below the fourth grade level. Both the secondary and post-secondary levels are struggling with students who cannot read adequately, and testing is being "dumbed down" to allow students to graduate from high school. Nevada set its cutting line for graduation at the point that 85 percent of the senior classes would be eligible.

THE SKUNK AT THE GARDEN PARTY: HIGH SCHOOL ALGEBRA

Why this analogy? The very word "skunk" evokes shudders and avoidance. At a garden party or any other social activity, the appearance of a skunk can be guaranteed not only to scatter the guests in every direction but to end the affair as well. Unfortunately, the word "math," and more specifically, "algebra," can elicit exactly the same behavior from students whose preparation may be shaky or close to non-existent.

A real democracy for all can be created by a nation whose citizens can read and write and where a large and economically stable middle class exists, a philosophy the United States has maintained since its creation.

But now, as reported by *The Washington Post* analyst, E. J. Dionne, Jr., a couple of new elements must be added to this philosophy because of the society in which we live.[8] Co-authors, Robert Moses, a Harvard-trained

mathematician, and Charles Cobb, of *Radical Equations,* advance the thesis
that

> The most urgent social issue affecting poor people and people of color is eco-
> nomic access. In today's world, economic access and full citizenship depend
> crucially on math and science literacy . . . Verbal literacy . . . is no longer
> enough. Algebra, once solely in place as the gatekeeper for higher math and
> the priesthood who gained access to it, now is the gatekeeper for citizenship;
> and people who don't have it are like the people who couldn't read and write
> in the Industrial Age.

These two authors are not alone. Cited in an earlier article of *The
Washington Post,* another educator, Montgomery County (Maryland) Public
Schools Superintendent Jerry Weast, spoke out on the issue as well, upon
finding out that: "Two-thirds of the students in the county taking the
Algebra I final exam in January [2000] flunked. The failure rate was 80 per-
cent among black and Hispanic students."[9] He told Staff Writer Brigid
Schulte, " 'I don't want 60 percent of my students failing the exam. . . . No
algebra exam means no SAT test. No SAT test means limited college choice.' "
The article further pointed out: "Algebra is the gateway to college and higher
paying careers in a new technical world." An even stronger statement was
made by Lee Metcalf, president of the National Council of Teachers of
Mathematics, who stated in the same article: " 'Algebra is the civil rights
issue of the new millennium, because it's that critical.' "

However, the Montgomery County public education system's problem
with algebra is not unique: much the same situation prevails in other
school systems, both urban and suburban. The "quick-fix" solutions
tried by Montgomery County have not worked for the system as a whole:
smaller class sizes, beginning the algebra course earlier than the ninth
grade, teacher training, and setting a very low passing score for the algebra exam. This last tactic was criticized by Roscoe Nix, president of the
local chapter of the NAACP, as constituting "educational fraud." He
added, "I'm not saying the school system practices apartheid. But the
results of this test suggest that these children are placed in an educational
apartheid system."

While Nix's "suggestion" was not directly addressed, Weast did appoint a
kind of special investigator to examine the algebra problem in the Montgomery
County school system and to review the test scores of approximately 10,000
freshmen in 1999–2000. The results were dismaying. She subsequently
reported: " 'There clearly seems to be a level of demarcation that separates

white and Asian students into higher levels of math earlier . . . We have to take an honest look at why. . . . We have to figure out how we got here so we can undo what we did.' "[10] Not surprisingly, the analysis of the test scores reflected the following differences. Whites and Asians typically did well on the test; blacks and Hispanics, when they did take algebra, typically did not. Again, this pattern is echoed in other school districts coping with diverse populations.

Now what about *this* situation? Moses answers first by saying "education is rooted in the culture of today's students [or] many will walk away."[11] But then he says more is needed. And he applies his civil rights experience to the problem, saying the solution must come from both top and bottom in the society. That is, an articulate and dedicated commitment to "self-help" from the affected groups at the "bottom" must be mounted that forces a recognized political obligation on the part of society to redress the situation from the top.[12] And in a kind of variation on this theme, Schulte reported on an experiment running at the Paint Branch High School that is diverse and "relatively poor" (one third of its enrollment), where 65 percent of the students passed the algebra test. This rate was close to the passing rate of much more posh schools in the county. The teachers offered the following explanation:

> There is no magic wand. . . . Just hard work. They meet before and after school to tutor students. They teach struggling students two periods of algebra a day. They make up to 600 calls a year to parents of algebra students, asking why they missed class or didn't do their homework. So what do the teachers themselves say is the problem?
>
> There's just so many things that a kid's got to know to do algebra, and just don't, said [one] teacher . . . after a painstaking class on the quadratic formula, used to trace the arc of a projected object, like a baseball. "I wish they knew how to add, multiply, subtract and divide fractions. That's where we get bogged down."[13]

Teachers applaud the goal of getting more students into algebra. But, they say, start early and do more to prepare students before they walk into a ninth-grade algebra class.

> One teacher who asked not to be named noted that if students take Algebra I in the ninth grade without the likelihood of being successful, they can wind up hating math. Taking algebra later does not close the door on a student.[14]

We couldn't agree more—readiness is critical. But there is another element that must be looked at here, and that is the nature of the ninth grade itself.

About eight years ago, we contacted then D.C. Schools Superintendent Franklin Smith about running a research study involving "at risk" youth at the junior or senior levels in high school. The project called for using computer software productivity training as a "hook" to interest these students in postsecondary education. After listening to us and what we proposed to do, he asked if it would be possible to operate the project at the ninth grade level since the ninth grade was a "do or die proposition" for these students and the school system suffered its greatest number of dropouts at this level. Unfortunately, he did not follow through and, therefore, nothing was done. More recently, the same problem at the ninth grade level was pointed out by other researchers studying the situation in inner city high schools across the country, where Philadelphia's schools constituted one example.

> By [ninth grade] then, teachers traditionally have expected them [the students] to have mastered basic reading and math skills. . . . High schools also often fail to attend to the social problems students confront when they arrive, including the more free-flowing high school atmosphere. Researchers in Philadelphia found that students frequently fail more classes in ninth than in eighth, and attendance plummets. . . . [And finally, still another researcher notes:] "Ninth grade is a life-and-death situation for these [minority] children."[15]

While problems with reading have long been recognized, only lately are the ones with math really being considered. *The New York Times*'s reporter Zernike noted that at the present time, only 13 of the 50 states require algebra for high school graduation.[16] In our own experiences as professors, we have known that proficiency in reading, writing, and algebra are critical to success in college. Moreover, algebra is the ascendant course if a student wants to pursue an academic degree and career in engineering, mathematics or the sciences.

In regard to preparing students for algebra, memorization of basic facts that will expedite learning of it has become a dirty word to many school officials and sometimes to the general public as well. As recently as May 14, 2001, school officials and some parents in Fairfax County, Virginia, squabbled over the teaching of math and selection of arithmetic textbooks. The debate over teaching math can be epitomized by the statement, "with math, the question is, should students memorize formulas and multiplication tables or learn them though illustrative problems?"[17]

Why are we talking about an *either—or* situation? Why aren't we talking about an *and* situation?

This debate has continued because politicians and others, who may not know anything about teaching math, keep the debate going to earn brownie points with the voters. An illustration of this *either—or* situation was provided in an article citing Fairfax County Superintendent, Daniel Domenech, who said, "I would submit that this [*either—or* situation] is political demagoguery. . . . It is an attempt to politicize education that has nothing to do with students and learning."[18]

Memorization has earned a bad reputation because people who criticize it have not taken the time to really understand either the meaning of the word "memorization" or to understand its benefits. The dictionary meaning of the word memorization is "committing to memory," and arithmetic facts can be committed to memory by practice and continuing exposure to situations. Another situation not clearly understood and analyzed by individuals who criticize memorization is the fact that calculators, when not used judiciously, can slow down students' work, and not help them at all. There are at least three reasons why students should be able to carry out arithmetic operations in their heads without having to resort to a calculator. First, students need to understand the meaning of the arithmetic operations. Second, students need to know intuitively whether the final answer is correct or not from the "order of magnitude" point of view, e.g., what is the answer for $10^5/10^{-6}$? The student who does not understand the arithmetical operation and who does not have a feel for order of magnitude is likely to use the calculator incorrectly and may obtain an answer of 10^{-1} and then insist that the answer is correct because the calculator was used in obtaining the answer. On the other hand, the student who does understand the arithmetical operations will realize instantly that it only involves the addition of two single digit numbers and the final answer is 10^{11}. Third, it is very time-consuming to do simple arithmetic functions with a calculator, like multiplying two single-digit numbers, particularly when there are a lot of them.

In addition, you cannot teach algebra to high school students if they constantly require the use of a calculator to do basic arithmetical operations ($-4 + 11$ or 6 times 9). Similarly, you cannot teach science courses if every time students encounter a quadratic equation, they have to consult a book for the formula to solve that equation. And, of course, you cannot teach advanced courses in math, science, and engineering if students are unable to recognize patterns like, $x^2 - y^2 = (x - y) * (x + y)$. Once understood, these basic facts must be committed to memory, and that's that. If such facts were memorized, students would be faster in solving quantitative problems. Those who favor the "new math" may fail to realize that arithmetic skills are required to solve any quantitative problem. Even in new math, more time will be available to teach the techniques for problem solving if, and only if, basic arithmetic facts are on the fingertips of students. That is, the facts have been committed to memory. In summary, we must realize that memorization of basic quantitative facts and use of these facts to solve quantitative problems is both integral parts of learning math and science. So, why are we proposing an intellectual divorce?

ACHIEVEMENT TESTING

Four questions are of paramount importance when one deals with achievement testing. What is the purpose of the test? What is actually being tested? How adequate are the results obtained? How are the results being used? When we examine achievement tests, such as the *Stanford Achievement Tests,* the *Iowa Tests of Basic Skills,* the *Virginia Standard of Learning* (SOLS), the *Maryland State Achievement Performance* (MSAPs), the *National Assessment of Educational Progress* (NAEP), and a myriad of other tests, the answer to the first question is clear. These tests are designed to measure student achievement at various grade levels in various areas of the curriculum, such as reading, science, social studies and mathematics. However, what the uninformed user does not realize is that every one of these tests involves only *a limited sample* of the kinds of knowledge and skills presumably being taught at the particular grade level(s) involved. In other words, achievement tests do *not* cover everything that is being taught at the respective grade level(s). Moreover, the tests vary in the content covered, item construction, the size, type, selection and location of the standardization or norm group(s) used, scoring procedures, etc.

If the answer to the first question is a bit murky, the plot really thickens when we try to answer the second question. Some people would claim that it is really reading comprehension that is being tested. Some would argue that it is test-taking skill or the knowledge of test construction that is being tested. Others would ask if it is the quality of the academic programs and the home background advantages of the students that are really being tested, thus questioning if a particular test discriminates against students on ethnic and/or economic grounds. Many others would challenge the fairness of a test in terms of its coverage of curriculum area, e.g., the ninth grade English program in an affluent Michigan suburb versus an analogous curriculum in a remote poverty area of the Mississippi delta. Finally, achievement tests are often sparse in the numbers of reasoning and extrapolation questions included, because such questions are very difficult to design in comparison with those involving fact and detail, and the tests furnish no ways of assessing creative potential, leadership ability, and so forth.

Politicians in their zeal to address the crisis in public education have practically ignored the answer to the third question. In assessing the adequacy of any achievement test results for a group, it must be borne in mind that these results are like a posed snapshot of people. That is, the results are only a limited look at these people at a particular instant in time. Moreover, while achievement tests results generally do tend to be accurate for *groups over time,* assuming that the conditions for testing are adequate, the students are motivated, and the test has been properly administered and scored, the results are often not either particularly accurate for a single individual at any given time or for the overall group in the short run, like three years.

Moreover, the language for reporting the results is often confusing. For example, to say that a student in the tenth grade is "reading two standard deviations below the mean" of a given test has a fuzzy meaning for most parents, teachers and principals, except that it is a poor score. If the score is translated to mean "Below Basic," as is the case with the *Stanford 9,* the meaning is still fuzzy. However, if this phrase is equated to the reading skills comparable to those of the average third grader, only then does the meaning become loud and clear, and threatening for the schools.

The results of an achievement test can be broken down into assessing the performance of a school district at specified grade levels, as well as by gender, by ethnic group, etc. Such assessments can also be carried out by individual schools at each grade level. But all of these interpretations are only as good as the test itself, the conditions under which the test was administered (e.g., if the kids don't care, an external event intrudes, or the procedures for administering the test are violated), the accuracy of the scoring, and the equivalence of the norm group for the test to the students who are being tested. If the norm group(s) involved is very different from the particular student(s) taking the test, then the results obtained are highly questionable, if not downright worthless.

In an article in *The Washington Post,* an unpublished study by the Rand Corporation "found that 50 percent to 80 percent of the improvement in a school's average test scores from year to year is related to random factors rather than to real gains in learning."[19] Add to this another report in *The Washington Post* that documented the resistance of eighth graders in Montgomery County, Maryland, to having to take MSPAP tests.[20] These students knew full well the importance of the test results to their schools and staffs, if not to themselves, and their general attitude was simply not to take the test seriously, since the results would not have any effect on them.

The answer to the fourth question is fraught with peril at the present time. The uses of achievement test results have been pushed far beyond rational applications. A new term has even been coined for this strange extension: "high-stakes testing." In school districts from New York to California, "parents have led boycotts of state-mandated exams, contending that high-stakes [tests] lead to simple-minded reform."[21] Already, teachers are complaining about having to drop parts of their classroom programs, like art and music and creative writing, in order to spend time schooling students to take the tests. Testing scandals are being reported, where teachers have given instruction in the actual items of the tests to be used. Such reports, when compared with the legitimate uses of testing and the *caveats* that must be considered in their use for decision-making purposes, make Mr. Paige's statement, cited in the following paragraph, look ridiculous—particularly the "irrefutable data" part.

Achievement testing has now become the hottest issue in education. According to current political wisdom, all schools have to do is increase the amount of achievement testing, punish the staffs of the failing schools, and then these schools will become accountable. Seemingly in support of this view is Education Secretary Roderick R. Paige who "has called frequent testing the key element in improving education. 'There is no logic in not knowing where a student is. . . . Tests provide irrefutable data about which kids are learning what, and in which classrooms.' "[22] Completely lacking in this avowed cause and effect relationship is any mention of variations in the classroom program, quality of teaching, differences in the achievement tests themselves, attitudes and academic preparation of the students taking the tests, etc. The new education legislation, the *Leave No Child Behind Act of 2002*, has as its centerpiece a major testing program for grades 3 through 8. The results of the tests are to be used to penalize low-performing schools that fail to show major improvement over a five-year period. While there is some emphasis on providing money for the teaching of reading and for teacher preparation, by and large, the "wisdom" undergirding this legislation seems to be that if we test children often enough, they will somehow improve their achievement levels. Testing alone cannot possibly upgrade achievement even if students take the tests so often that they memorize the questions, have enough time to look up the answers in between trials, or teachers actually teach the test under the guise of preparing the students to handle the test's format and time pressures. What seems to have escaped both politicians and educators in pushing this legislation through is the teaching of the program on which the tests should be based. But then, the cost of testing programs is bargain basement cheap in comparison with upgrading teacher training and salaries, facts that were clearly pointed out by M. Sokolove in *The Washington Post*'s follow-up story to the testing scandal in Silver Spring, Maryland. Sokolove cited H. D. Hoover, principal author of *Iowa Tests of Basic Skills,* who noted that the tests " 'were never intended to be used as a hammer on teachers and school administrators.' He further commented that '[the tests] are incredibly inexpensive . . . compare $5-a-kid with what it would take to raise teachers' salaries to compete for the brightest college graduates. . . . The politicians like the tests because if you're for more tests, you can advocate for education without having to spend real money.' "[23]

But the Congress and the White House have marched on, and a big batch of kids in the third through the eighth grades are going to have to bear the brunt of the latest political effort to get tough about educational reform, by golly! Why are children having to bear the burden of accountability for the quality of their education? No child comes to school in the expectation of failing. It's the adults and communities who are failing the children. In our opinion, the whole accountability issue that is resting its case on achievement testing is just another instance of blaming the victim, of putting effects before causes. Whatever happened to teaching in this equation, to treating and paying teachers as professionals, to strengthening teacher-training programs, and to training teachers how to teach their disciplines to our increasingly diverse population?

Even if testing were the real answer, what test possibly can be used nationally that will effect educational accountability (reform) across 50 states? At this time, the *National Assessment of Educational Progress* probably comes the closest. So, what *is* educational accountability at a given grade level, such as the third? Should every third grade child be performing on the tests at the so-called third grade level in every subject? What about the immigrant child who has just arrived in the school and doesn't speak two words of English, the poverty child who is too exhausted or too hungry to keep awake during the testing session, or the gifted child who is already reading at the eighth grade level?

One thing is for sure: the testing companies are going to have a bonanza, but the effort is simplistic at best and is unlikely to achieve the reform being sought. A warning about the simplistic notion of achievement testing being the primary solution to the problem of educational reform comes from Harvard University's Civil Rights Project, which has just released its latest report, *"Schools More Separate: Consequence of a Decade of Resegregation."* The report provides evidence of "a return toward segregation in the K-to-12 grades despite a growing diversity of the general population and support for integration in public opinion surveys." Codirector of the project, Professor Gary Orfield also is reported as saying "that efforts by the White House and Congress to toughen school accountability through annual testing would probably backfire, driving minority children in failing schools to repeat grades and eventually drop out." Moreover, the report points out that resegregation "is contributing to a growing gap between the schools being attended by white students and those serving a large proportion of minority students." Also noted is that the average minority child (African American and Hispanic) typically attends those schools classified as "high-poverty schools."[24] Repeated achievement testing is going to improve the performance of these students?

As a postscript to this section, we note that the controversy about universities and colleges using or not using the *Scholastic Aptitude Test* as part of their admissions criteria has more or less faded from the scene. Since the use of this upper-level achievement test is a voluntary matter for higher education institutions, it has escaped the attention of the politicians. There are problems here, too, but nothing on the scale of magnitude of the problems at the elementary and secondary levels.

SURVIVING THE COLLEGE FRESHMAN YEAR

The adjustment to the freshman year of college is a major one. Only a scant three months previously, most first-year students in a college or university were in structured high school programs, living at home, and receiving guidance from parents. In high school most of these students would have experienced relatively small classes, anywhere from 8 to 25 students.

Now, upon arriving at most public and some private higher education institutions, the new students find the situation drastically changed. A new freedom is given to students; large classes in freshman subjects are common, typically from 300 to 600 students; and the professors who teach are often remote and overburdened. In addition, many students are told early in the freshman year, at orientation or in large classes, "Look to your left, look to your right, one of you will not be back next year," signaling that a fair number of students will wash out of these classes. This is still happening. A large number of students, sometimes in excess of 80 percent in the science and engineering courses, either fail or drop out of these courses. Not only is this situation occurring in science courses, it is quite prevalent in other courses as well. As reported by Linda Perlste:

Part of the problem is that introductory freshman courses in many American colleges are taught by weary and overburdened political science and biology professors who think their role in life is to protect the legal and medical professions from incompetents. They feel they are saving the world from future malpractice suits by flunking as many students as possible.[25]

Establishing large classes at the freshman level began as an administrative device during the 1960s and 1970s, to accommodate the large influx of students who were entering higher education. The device was cost efficient in several ways: it reduced staffing costs; in the case of public institutions it could be used to assure state formula funding; and it practically guaranteed that large numbers of students would wash out, thereby reducing the student body to a manageable size in subsequent courses. These points are well documented in a recent survey by John Gardner, executive director of the Policy Center on the First Year of College at Brevard College in North Carolina who observed:

[Freshman] students reported that "extensive lecturing" was the most prevalent teaching technique they encountered with 96% saying it was used "frequently" or "occasionally". At the same time, it was ranked last among methods they preferred, with only 21.4% finding it "very important" to their course work. Mr. Gardner concludes that the large lecture format is a symptom of colleges that view freshmen as a "cash cow," . . . I think that does our students an injustice. I think they want more than just the facts.[26]

Even for the well-prepared and self-disciplined student, the freshman year is fraught with peril. But for the student who is not so well prepared, motivated or self-disciplined—and many freshmen, no matter how potentially able they are, have these characteristics—the stage is set for failure. We have long known that small class sizes are valuable for student learning at the elementary and secondary levels. Why should small class sizes not be equally valuable at the postsecondary level as well? The elite private institutions have always known this fact. Perhaps it is time that we stop looking at the freshman students as "cash cows" and start looking at them as valued members of the oncoming generation, who need to be educated.

However, huge classes, increased freedom, shaky self-discipline and diminished supervision are not the only perils confronting the freshman student. A hidden danger is the difficulty of the content itself. The social studies of the high school suddenly transmogrifies itself into distinct subject matter areas, such as history, political science, psychology and sociology, all of which are packed with their own concepts, research, perspectives and theories. Much of the information has little relevance to the students' own lives, particularly those who are poor or minority students. Then, too, the 50-minute academic hour that is typical of the freshman year courses in the humanities, social sciences, and math barely provides time to cover the content, let alone allow for a student to receive special help during the class period. As a faculty member, Hughes consistently advised first-semester freshman students who also were in the developmental courses in English, reading or math to avoid the heavy reading courses, like sociology and the other social sciences, until they had, at least, successfully completed the remedial courses. Hughes also was commissioned by UDC to carry out a retention tracking study using transcripts from one group of freshmen for a four-semester period. Randomly selected, all but a tiny few of these students had been required to take no fewer than two developmental courses upon their entry into the university. The attrition rate of the approximately 250 students studied was 60 percent, of which 90 percent were gone by the end of the freshman year. However, the most interesting finding was that the "survivors" had, for the most part, found ways of easing their first and second semesters of college work by self-selecting those courses that did not overwhelm them with heavy reading, but still met various university-wide requirements. Among these self-selected freshman courses were Public Speaking, Music Appreciation, Art Appreciation, Health and Physical Education, and a sophomore introductory course in psychology that had short units, sections on definitions and lots of illustrations. Although not a university requirement, the students often selected the keyboarding course offered in the School of Business. Not until the third semester did these students seriously begin the heavy reading courses.

NOTES

1. *Immigration and Naturalization Service Yearbook,* 1998, p. 22.
2. Canedy, D. (2001, March 25). Troubling Label for Hispanics: Girls Most Likely to Drop Out. *The New York Times,* p. NE19.
3. Canedy, D. (2001, March 25). Troubling Label for Hispanics: Girls Most Likely to Drop Out. *The New York Times,* p. NE19.
4. McWhorter, J. H. (2000). *Losing the Race.* New York: The Free Press, pp. vii–xv.
5. Raspberry, W. (2000, May 12). They Never Learn. *The Washington Post,* p. A47.

6. King, C. (2001, March 31). They Just Can't Read. *The Washington Post,* p. A21.

7. King, C. (2001, March 31). They Just Can't Read. *The Washington Post,* p. A21.

8. Dionne, E. J. (2001, March 6). Into the Math Mix. *The Washington Post,* Editorial section.

9. Schulte, B. (2000, May 9). Montgomery Tries to Solve Math Problem. *The Washington Post,* p. B1.

10. Schulte, B. (2000, May 9). Montgomery Tries to Solve Math Problem. *The Washington Post,* p. B1.

11. Dionne, E. J. (2001, March 6). Into the Math Mix. *The Washington Post,* Editorial section.

12. Dionne, E. J. (2001, March 6). Into the Math Mix. *The Washington Post,* Editorial section.

13. Schulte, B. (2000, May 9). Montgomery Tries to Solve Math Problem. *The Washington Post,* p. B1.

14. Fletcher, M. (2001, March 3). Progress on Dropout Rate Stalls. *The Washington Post,* p. A1.

15. Fletcher, M. (2001, March 3). Progress on Dropout Rate Stalls. *The Washington Post,* p. A1.

16. Zernike, K. (2001, April 15). Why Johnny Can't Read, Write, Multiply or Divide. *The New York Times,* p. WK-5.

17. Seymour, L. (2001, May 14). How Math is Taught Has Fairfax Squabbling. *The Washington Post.* p. B1.

18. Seymour, L. (2001, May 14). How Math is Taught Has Fairfax Squabbling. *The Washington Post.* p. B1.

19. Fletcher, M. (2001, July 9). As Stakes Rise, School Groups Put Exams to the Test. *The Washington Post.* p. A1.

20. Johnson, D. (2001, April 30). Maryland's 8th-grade Whatevers: MSPAP Exam Faces Teens' Indifference, *The Washington Post,* p. B1.

21. Fletcher, M. (2001, July 9). As Stakes Rise, School Groups Put Exams to the Test. *The Washington Post.* p. A1.

22. Fletcher, M. (2001, July 9). As Stakes Rise, School Groups Put Exams to the Test. *The Washington Post.* p. A1.

23. Sokolove, M., (2002, February 24). True or False? *The Washington Post Magazine.* p. 23.

24. Schemo, D. J. (2001, July 20). U.S. Schools Turn More Segregated, a Study Finds. *The New York Times.* p. A12.

25. (2001, July 22). The Education Review, TRUST, *The Washington Post, The Washington Post Magazine.* p. 20.

26. Brownstein, A. (2000, November 17). With the Aim of Retaining Freshmen, a Survey Examines Their Experience. *The Chronicle of Higher Education,* p. A71.

5

TEACHING DILEMMA IN THIS DECADE

Society gets what it pays for and what it values. In the United States, we have not treated the teaching profession in the same way that we have such professions as computer science, engineering, and law in either pay or respect. We have let public school systems deteriorate, have allowed substandard conditions to prevail in personnel, equipment, and material for large numbers of our schools, and have clung to obsolete notions of compensation and training for our teachers. Yet we want future generations to be adequately prepared.

In the previous chapter, we examined the classroom in which teaching must occur and the education takes place. In this chapter, we focus on the professionals who are—and will be—teaching the enormously diverse population who now characterize American society. Education is, at last, being recognized and is, perhaps, on its way to being accepted *finally* as the key profession that it is. At the heart of education is the teacher, and the time has come to examine what teachers face right now and future teachers will continue to face in this first decade of the new millennium. We begin with an assessment of the current situation in today's classrooms.

TEACHER SHORTAGE—BIG-TIME

Lately, schools all over the country are facing a severe teacher shortage. This problem has been lurking on the horizon for a long time, but it has now moved onto our front door step. The traditional pool of women teachers, usually single, for whom other professions were almost closed and who were paid meager wages, is history. In short, quality on the cheap is long gone. Married women teachers' salaries have been traditionally viewed as a secondary income in the family, a perception that lingers even today.

The U.S. Department of Education is predicting a shortage of 2.5 million teachers for the next decade. Along with this general shortage, the agency is also predicting a shortage of approximately 500,000 teachers in math, science, English, and some foreign languages. This shortage cannot be masked any longer; it must be dealt with. However, the impending shortage is no longer just a numbers game of putting live bodies in classrooms—serious in and of itself; it has also now become a deadly serious matter about finding enough teachers to staff the classrooms. In the inner cities, rural areas, and now even in the suburbs, public school systems are vying with one another to find what is increasingly becoming an *avis rara:* the teacher who is content expert, knows how to teach in diverse educational settings, and is willing to be paid much less, in comparison with other high-demand professionals.

For a long time, at the high school level urban schools have masked the problem of teacher shortages in a content area, such as math, by pressuring a teacher in a so-called related area, like biology, to teach math, a subject in which that teacher was not qualified. A teacher who is only minimally content-qualified in a new subject can be only minimally effective. The result is that both the teacher and the students are shortchanged. When the practice is widespread, the society is shortchanged as well.

Because of the escalating shortage, a new variation of this practice now consists of just putting adults who can read and write but have little or no orientation in the teaching profession into unstaffed classrooms. This is known as the "live body" approach. Such individuals may or may not have baccalaureate degrees. Usually, these adults don't remain, even though many of them are interested in a career change and often take cuts in pay in order to try out teaching. Again, such persons, who with some help might have developed into teachers, are lost to the profession, and the shortchanging process continues.

But that's not the only problem: beginning, baccalaureate-level teachers are struggling to make a living. Last year an article pointed out that teachers are scrambling to make ends meet in the affluent communities where they teach. For example, "the median household income in Washington and its suburban counties ranges from $43,000 in the District to close to $90,000 in Fairfax County. The starting salary for a teacher with a bachelor's degree usually falls below $35,000."[1] Housing alone becomes a major problem. A year later, the situation remains the same.

We suspect that a similar situation prevails in many urban and suburban communities. What this means is that the teachers have to find other jobs to supplement their incomes, and, in turn, they may have to cut corners in their teaching and either delay or forfeit furthering their own education. Or they select another option. If the situation becomes too much, they leave the classroom altogether. As a footnote, the 2001 session of the Virginia Assembly refused to pass a bill that would have allowed the counties and cities of the state to decide individually if they wanted to add an additional half penny to the local sales tax to support education. The Assembly would have passed the half penny for transportation, but not the half penny for education.

Recently, in an article in *The New York Times*, Vartan Gregorian, President of the Carnegie Corporation, said this shortage of teachers is more a function of retention rather than lack of interest:

> America has no shortage of idealistic and competent people who want to teach. Far from it: the nation's 1,300 schools of education have more than enough teachers in training to meet the need. So why should this be an issue at all? Because 30 percent of all our teachers and up to 50 percent of teachers in urban schools leave their jobs within five years. Out of every 600 students entering four-year programs, only 180 complete them, only 72 become teachers and only about 40 are still teaching several years later.[2]

So, what's the problem here? There is no one problem but a panoply of problems. Among them are tolerating insufficient public and official support, subscribing to "the misconception that anyone can teach [that] exists throughout the education system," and allowing schools of education to become cash cows, playing numbers games of their own and watering down programs in order to survive. Other problems include raiding other nations' teachers, trusting our children to marginal conditions, and issuing 'emergency' teaching licenses to unprepared applicants—a practice that would not be tolerated in any other profession."[3]

As a society, we have clung to a "Goodbye, Mr. Chips" mentality in order to allow us hypocritically to proclaim the value of great teaching, becoming misty-eyed over the wonderful teachers *we* have had—but to pay neither respect nor money to those who teach our children.

CHAPTER 5

THE EIGHT-HUNDRED POUND GORILLA: CURRENT HIGH SCHOOL AND POSTSECONDARY TEACHER PREPARATION

In addition to teacher shortages, big city public school systems also face another problem: the quality of the teachers being hired. Increasingly, these systems are looked at as hardship posts; well-qualified teachers have choices. And the D.C. Public Schools are no exception. Colbert King characterized the D.C. Public Schools as "a broken system of education." He asked Superintendent of Schools, Paul Vance about teacher quality, who responded by saying that "the District has hired second-rate teachers 'who could not get jobs anyplace else,' especially in the Montgomery County School system, where he previously served as superintendent." Moreover, Vance stated, "that in the District historically you haven't had A-tier teachers, . . . only B- and low-grade C-tier teachers." Finally, he blasted the schools as being a "system without a curriculum" and lacking "the collective instructional intelligence to manage and supervise what it is we are doing."[4]

A statement similar to that of Superintendent Vance was made by Harold O. Levy, Chancellor of the New York City Public Schools:

> The quality of teachers has been declining for decades, and no one wants to talk about it. Principals know the truth and have to deal with it as best they can, but unions are reluctant to admit weaknesses in any of their members, colleges are loath to acknowledge the poor quality of their education programs, and administrators are afraid that confronting the problem will further erode confidence in public education.[5]

Vance's and Levy's comments could probably be applied to virtually every other big city school system in the country.

Another problem that has been well known in educational circles is the generally low opinion in which most colleges of education are held, largely because of lack of rigor in their teacher preparation course offerings. This problem has now become known to the general public as well. Overall, the criticism is directed at the watering down of content—what is to be taught, and at the overemphasis on pedagogy—how that content is to be taught. Acknowledging these criticisms, Vartan Gregorian, President of the Carnegie Corporation, noted:

> We lack a critical mass of very good schools of education. Many colleges and universities have marginalized their schools of education, treating them as revenue generators. Survival for these schools has often meant increasing enrollments and reducing educational quality.[6]

A related problem has to do with teacher certification. Increasingly, state certification is being seen as an obstacle to the recruiting of talented and qualified professionals into the field of teaching. In this regard, Patrick Welsh, an English teacher in Alexandria, Virginia, reported that a colleague had noted, "Virginia's certification system is totally blind and has nothing to do with good teaching . . . reminding me how little the education classes . . . being required have to do with anything that goes on in the classroom."[7]

The business-as-usual approach to teacher training has already proven that it is simply not going to work. The major teacher shortage in many school systems is too critical. The traditional approach involves what one teacher has called a " 'minimum competency' mentality that dumbs down both teaching and learning." Part of this dumbing-down is accomplished by the sheer passage of time required for the program—the whole process takes time, time, and more time. The teacher-to-be takes the required number of courses in content, pedagogy for teaching that content and other miscellaneous preparatory courses, and the state certification agency finally determines, "Now you are a teacher."

Then the follow-on occurs: the new teacher arrives in the classroom and is given the "prescription" for exactly what is to be taught, when it is to be taught, and in what ways, so that the curriculum is unsullied by the teacher's mind. Only in education are beginners expected to perform at the same level as their more experienced colleagues. The prescription approach is designed by textbook publishers and their education consultants to bridge the gap between the novice and the veteran teacher. In part, the prescription approach is designed to assure that new teachers can hit the ground running, just like their more experienced colleagues. However, the down side of the approach is that it can prevent the newcomer from really teaching the students whom he or she faces, because a uniform prescription only works in certain situations. Also, when the teacher is not really comfortable in the situation, the prescription approach can be initially helpful, but the risk exists that the teacher will not adapt the content to the students and will, instead, hide behind the prescription or invoke its corollary: the students aren't prepared. Certainly, alert teachers do recognize this dilemma. Unfortunately, the prescription approach applies not only to new teachers; it persists and is currently being expanded. Its latest application can be seen in the sudden hysteria about "standards," i.e., limiting the curriculum solely to what will appear on tests, and then repeatedly testing the students to death at the middle school and high school levels and calling the process "preparation."

However, when the secondary teacher is content-qualified (i.e., holds at least a bachelor's degree with a major in the content area), then the prescription approach can stifle any creativity such a teacher may have in reaching out to students. Individuals of this type frequently come into teaching from another route than the teachers colleges and have a great desire to teach—often taking cuts in pay to do so.

One other practice that needs to be mentioned is the standard operating procedure in the treatment of new teachers, who usually pull the most "challenging" (code word for "worst") teaching environments a particular school district has to offer because of the seniority system that prevails in selecting teaching assignments. Challenging environments usually are a combination of old buildings; dilapidated equipment and materials; a teaching staff of "old-timers," who often have merely accommodated themselves to the system and do not want anybody rocking the boat; overwhelmed beginners or makeshift hires, who are trying to learn (or, in the worst case scenario, just filling in to maintain law and order and collect a paycheck); and students who, for whatever reasons, are seriously underprepared academically. Mentoring and assistance are normally minimal in these settings, and it becomes a case of sink or, more likely, get out of the pool and never come back.

If a teacher rises to greatness in the classroom, given the impediments just described, it is a miracle akin to the Second Coming!

At the postsecondary level, a terminal degree in the discipline from an accredited institution is the primary ticket for employment. In four-year institutions, a graduate degree in a specialized particular subject is required. Community colleges, depending upon the subject to be taught, often put more emphasis on experience. In these settings, students pass the word to each other when great teaching does take place, but it is certainly not a phenomenon that receives recognition from peers or the academic administrators in the institution.

TYPES OF TEACHERS AND THE "GREAT DISCONNECT"

A phenomenon we have termed the "great disconnect" consists of the students and the teacher not being on the same wavelength with regard to the particular subject matter being taught. The great disconnect happens in one of two ways. In one of them, the teacher, who really does know the subject matter, is not communicating the subject matter to the students in ways they can understand. In the other case, the teacher, who has a shallow grasp of the subject matter, finds ways to mask the lack of knowledge when in front of the class. In the first case, the students are learning something, but not the subject that the teacher is teaching. In the second case, the students are being sidetracked. In both cases, the students are being cheated.

Until recently, curiously absent from the public statements about the causal factors of the disconnect has been the teacher. It is only in the last year or so that the teacher has begun to emerge into prominence as a key player, albeit a maligned one. Having let public education drift despite warnings that began as early as the 1960s and were reinforced with the publication of *A Nation at Risk* in 1983, the taxpaying public has suddenly awakened to the significance of lowered test scores and the teacher shortage as they are affecting *me* and *my kids*. Intuitively, the public really does know that the teacher *is* the key connecting link between children and the educative process. But paradoxically, a general perception held by the public, and by most professional educators as well, is that anyone can teach. What the public has been unwilling to face is that quality in teaching no longer comes cheap. And because of this unwillingness, the teaching profession has become prey to the types of teachers we describe here. That there are still great ones around is amazing.

Now let us look at the types of teachers currently in the public education system at the high school and college levels and see what their relationship is to the "great disconnect." Some of the types do better than others, of course.

One is a *fully content-qualified teacher in a particular discipline,* such as physics or math. However, the pedagogy of this teacher type is predominantly the rear-view, back-of-the-head lecture method, and the only entity that gets dazzled by the brilliance is the chalkboard. When the teacher finally turns around, it's to make the homework assignment—and then everyone evaporates at the bell. This type of teacher typically predominates at the postsecondary level, but is not as common at the high school level any more. Now, if for a moment we assume that all it takes to teach is content expertise, then there should be few dropouts. But how then do we explain an attrition rate of as high as 80 percent in certain disciplines at the college freshman level, despite the fact that we have all the experts we need with Ph.D.'s in their disciplines?

For example, the attrition rate in the Washington, D.C. school system between grades 9 and 12 is conservatively estimated at 40 percent. The same pattern is seen in the Philadelphia and New York public education systems at the secondary level. In higher education, the figures are harder to come by, because they typically remain in the individual institutions. But at the University of the District of Columbia, where the authors taught for many years, attrition during the first year has hovered around 70 percent, in spite of many sections of four remedial courses: two in math, one in English and the fourth in reading. And other public institutions are experiencing the same kinds of problems, according to information disclosed by colleagues at conferences and meetings. The National Center for Educational Statistics reports that 80 percent of the public institutions of higher education have at least one remedial course.

At the postsecondary level, teachers are almost always content-qualified in their disciplines—unless they have been peremptorily dumped into developmental (translation: remedial) courses in math, English and/or reading, which can begin at a fifth grade level. When teachers *do* teach in their disciplines at the freshman level, the problems typically lie in the pedagogy, the expanding diversity of the students, and the pressure from colleagues to conform to "tough standards" and flunk students who can't learn by the "teach-the-chalkboard" method. As students and later as professors, we have witnessed behaviors we consider detrimental to learning. First, in large lecture halls students nap, even when sitting in the first row. In smaller classes of 25–30, students have been observed to doze off peacefully in the back seats. Second, many professors copy, by and large, on the chalkboard either directly from the book or from their aged "yellow" notes. Third, after writing extensively on the chalkboard, professors often erase the board before students have a chance to take notes—let alone ask questions for clarification. In practice, most of these professors are "teaching the chalkboard." What the students are watching—if they attend at all—is the "virtuoso performance" of the professor.

To this, we add an example from our own experience. Over many years of teaching ethnically diverse and minority students, we achieved retention rates between 90 and 95 percent. Between 1981 and 1998, we also competed successfully for a number of grant-funded high-tech interventions from the U.S. Department of Education to improve the retention and success rates of minority students at the freshman and sophomore levels. These interventions involved not only us but also other professors. However, the situation of high dropout rates did not change in classes taught by other professors, a result that led us to examine our own teaching. Based on this examination, the experiences of more than 17 years and the continuing high dropout rate in many minority institutions, we concluded that it is the teacher who is the key element in students staying at or leaving postsecondary education. After all, in higher education, there is no truant officer or attendance counselor to roundup the "no-shows."

Subsequently, in 1995 and again in 1996, we submitted proposals to the Department of Education for retraining college faculty. Both times the proposals did not receive funding in spite of our successful record of obtaining funding with earlier projects and our own verified track record in teaching. These proposals clearly stated that faculty needed retraining in teaching their particular disciplines to non-traditional students. The peer review team, consisting of all faculty members, summarized their review by stating, "it [the proposal idea of faculty retraining] may not even be politically correct and it might be potentially explosive."[8]

More recently, in a study summarized by the National Science Foundation concerning students "Choosing and Leaving Science in Four Highly Selective Institutions," responses to a questionnaire by science majors showed that many of them found "the instruction to be 'too competitive,' to offer 'too few opportunities to ask questions,' and to be provided by professors who 'were relatively unresponsive, not dedicated, and not motivating.' " In short, they criticized "the instruction as inferior."[9]

Another study of seven institutions, summarized by the National Science Foundation, revealed that 90 percent of the students "who left science, mathematics, and engineering were concerned about pedagogy, i.e., poor teaching." "Inadequate advising or help with academic problems" was selected by approximately seven out of ten students. Interestingly, only four out of ten students reported that one of their reasons for leaving these areas was "inadequate high school preparation in basic subjects/study skills." In addition,

> Minority and majority students differed about their reasons for switching. Students of color tended to blame themselves for switching, whereas white students more often pointed to institutional failures. For example, white students complained of poor teaching and curriculum overload more than twice as often as did minority students.[10]

The unstated assumptions underlying these reports dealing with teaching techniques are that students are uniformly prepared and are responsible for their own learning; the professor's job is to transmit knowledge, and teaching need not be a priority for the professor. The students are not looked upon as active learners who want to maximize their own educative process rather than burn up all their energy trying to make sense of the teacher's presentation. Great teaching, unfortunately, is not usually a part of the reward system of colleges and universities. And in major university-wide requirements, such as math and English, considered as essential for most baccalaureate degrees, teachers are being increasingly required to use the prescription approach of secondary schools we described earlier in this chapter.

As professors, we have experienced many instances of such pressure from our colleagues to conform, when they saw differences in both our pedagogical techniques and student passing rates (close to 95 percent). For example, one of us used student work groups and collective responsibility in an introductory statistics course; the other used a technique requiring every single student to participate in solving each demonstration problem given in a freshman physics course. The students enrolled in these courses could have constituted case studies in diversity.

But terrific pedagogy alone is not the answer. There is the teacher who is *the pedagogical entertainer,* putting on a great floorshow for the students. But the "show" really may mask being only marginally qualified in the content, i.e., scrambling to stay one chapter ahead of the students or teaching one or two chapters of the book for the whole semester. This type is not uncommon at the high school level, and was characterized recently by Peggy Cooper Cafritz, the school board president of the D.C. Public Schools:

> We have a lot of [high school] teachers who are good teachers in terms of performance before a class. But they're not masters of their content [about 50 percent]. And so no matter how good you are at getting your point across, if you don't have the point, it doesn't matter.[11]

The implication here is that pedagogy without content mastery is insufficient for good teaching, and we certainly agree. Unfortunately, many people consider pedagogy as not being important at all. Zernike of *The New York Times,* reports, "In some cases, policy makers express near hostility to teacher education schools and note that the best private schools do not require teacher certification."[12] Of course, we hasten to note that if the students in the private schools are not handling a particular discipline, their parents find tutors for them post haste.

In a *New York Times* article, history of education professor, Jonathan Zimmerman, pointed out that potential (secondary) social studies teachers had as few as two courses in history, which was enough to be certified in Pennsylvania. Nationally, "about 54 percent of history students in grades

7 to 12 are taught by teachers who have neither a major nor a minor in history." He further noted that "the problem was even more acute in physics and chemistry, where more than 56 percent of the students [in these grades] have teachers who lack degrees in their subject areas." He pointed out that people who have never been trained adequately in a discipline can hardly be expected to teach others how to organize and interpret information (facts) in that discipline. Memorization of "raw facts" just won't do it.[13]

Another variation of the "great disconnect" is the teacher who is *a genuine mediocrity* or just plain marginal in terms of both subject matter and pedagogy. This teacher shows up, the students soon learn to shut up, the semester passes away, and another set of students disappears. Patrick Welsh's report of a colleague's comment epitomizes this kind of teacher very well. " 'The teaching profession is a breeding ground for mediocrity. You don't have to be exceptional . . . . There are so many teachers who are barely good enough. Public schools are the perfect place for people who are satisfied with getting by.' "[14]

All too often, this teacher type is the one (probably Vance's "Tier-C") students endure in the inner city classrooms. These people are hired because the school systems cannot attract top-flight candidates and a warm (supposedly) body has to stand before the students. *The New York Times* recently reported that in the New York City public school system between 30 and 40 percent of the teachers are from teacher education training institutions that are below any national ranking system. We doubt that the New York City system is alone in this regard.

The teachers' unions, with their emphasis on working conditions and pay and, until recently, their avoidance of quality and merit issues, probably have inadvertently contributed to the protection of *the genuine mediocrity*. This situation is beginning to change, as there are some recent instances of the unions working with teachers and administrators to improve the quality of teaching and programs. An example is the collaboration in the Montgomery County public schools. Hopefully, this approach will soon become a trend.

Students and a number of their parents in the poverty schools have long recognized another type of teacher who negatively affects them. Instances of this teacher have suddenly mushroomed on the increasingly diverse educational scene as well. This teacher can be termed *The "Reverse" Pygmalion*. Its significant characteristics can be variously described as cultural ignorance (putting the best face on it), cultural insensitivity and, sometimes, just plain prejudice (putting the worst face on it). Such characteristics are manifest in the teacher who stands before students from cultures or ethnic groups other than his or her own, including that of poverty, and simply fails to see a set of students hoping to learn and be helped. Teachers in this category do see a long list of deficits and deficiencies, often beginning with language. The teacher's perception is not limited to new arrivals in this country; it may also extend to social class, economic status, and/or ethnic groups as well. African Americans have been complaining about this situation for years. But whatever the specific culturally diverse reality is, *The Reverse Pygmalion* expects less achievement from certain students than from their "established" (middle and upper middle class) white or Asian peers, with the result that the teacher's level of effort drops as well. The students, even if they remain in the classroom, are shortchanged not only in terms of learning the subject matter, but also in terms of their own sense of self worth.

We surmise that these three types of teachers are contributing to the continued underpreparedness as shown by test scores and increased dropout rates in high school. In a desperate attempt to solve this problem, some school administrators have gone beyond the time honored summer make-up programs and have proposed a thirteenth year of schooling in order to do catch up. For example, this recommendation was supported by Warren Furutani and Jack Fujimoto.[15] This proposal is basically an administrative quick fix and sidesteps the problems of teacher preparation and student diversity. There is no evidence that adding extra time to graduation will prepare students better. On the contrary, adding the thirteenth year or extra months at the end of the twelfth year will cost more, but no numbers are available at the national level. Undoubtedly, such a practice would create further problems. This position has been well stated in a *Boston Globe* editorial, "[I]s the extended school year 'another quick and easy suggestion to cure schools?' Is more necessarily better?"[16] In this context, Diana Ravitch observed, "Students were staying in school longer than ever, but were they learning more than ever? Few thought so, nor did available evidence suggest that they were."[17] Prolonging graduation and offering courses during the summer are based on the student deficit model, where it is assumed that students can't learn the material during the regular four-year academic program. Also, these approaches have ignored the fact that the problem does not lie with the students not learning. Rather the problem is teachers who can't teach effectively. Allowing extra time only perpetuates the problem and makes it worse, because the educational enterprise would undoubtedly use the same unqualified teachers again and again during the summers, as well as during a thirteenth year of high school. Lately, the same concern was expressed by William Romey, a professor emeritus, St. Lawrence University, Canton, N.Y., who writes, "same books, same exercises, possibly the same teacher (where the problem may lie in the first place)."[18] More of the same is a sure recipe for failure.

ACHIEVING "SYNC"

Now we come to the individual who also is arriving on the educational scene in increasing numbers. This teacher is the person who usually *is* qualified in some other profession, has at least a baccalaureate degree, wants to make a change, genuinely wants to give teaching a go, and is often willing to take a cut in pay. (These are not the live body types.) These individuals are *Questers* They are seeking something more in life than what they're currently experiencing. One of the authors was a *Quester* in the Baltimore City Public Schools many years ago, and it was the major defining point in her choice of career.

All of them will try. Some of them will make it, but as one writer, also a high school teacher himself, put it, they will differ from the typical "teacher education mold."[19] They usually are prescription approach resisters, feeling their way in the situation that they face and ultimately developing their own approach. Some will rise to greatness. Some won't make it at all, but it won't be for lack of trying. At the high school level, they are usually content-qualified, and will try all kinds of ways to connect with their students regardless of who these students are. Their watchword becomes "Whatever works," including going back to school to receive the kind of training that they consider to be necessary.

One last type of teacher must be mentioned, the "great" teacher. Here, the magic occurs: the connect happens; the students come alive in their learning. This teacher is the one who prompts the statement, "Great teachers are born, not made." To which we emphatically respond, "Not so." The problem with the belief undergirding the statement is that it treats teaching as a seamless whole, when, in point of fact, it is made up of many, many different factors, all operating harmoniously like a great symphony orchestra in performance. Let us list several such factors: expertise in the subject matter; lots of physical energy; a passion for the subject matter to be taught and an absolute belief in its significance; a desire to communicate it; a genuine respect for students as worthy human beings; a recognition and appreciation of the differences among students in terms of their personalities, talents, and contributions to the teaching-learning situation; acceptance of the main responsibility for the students' learning (i.e., if the students didn't learn the material, "what did I do that didn't work?" and then reteaching that material); assuring participation by all of the students—not just the "swifties;" anchoring the new learning to something that the students can directly relate to; always challenging, but never intimidating; a belief in one's ability to communicate with other human beings; and so forth. The list goes on and on.

A person may have an aptitude for teaching, content mastery and a high energy level, but the fact of the matter is that *great teaching is learned behavior.* Mastery of, and continuing deepening insight into, the discipline is a given for this teacher, but the connect to the students—the leap of communicative fire—lies in the instructional or pedagogical adaptations of this teacher to the students to be taught. However, occasional "great" teachers sprinkled here and there in the educational system simply will not suffice.

So, what *do* we do about making certain that large numbers of teachers who really can teach their subject matters are placed in the secondary and postsecondary classrooms? Hit-or-miss ways of putting really qualified and promising teachers in the classrooms and then encouraging them to rise to greatness must be found. New kinds of people must be attracted into the teaching profession—people who are energetic, who are trained and current in their disciplines, who have idealism, optimism and a belief in their capacity to communicate, and who consider that for them to turn in a mediocre performance in anything is a cardinal sin. The marginal, mediocre, Reverse Pygmalions and the entertainers who just occupy classroom space must be encouraged to vacate. And for those teachers who are already in the system who care about students and their teaching—and many exist, there must be support and tangible recognition.

We further answer that both teacher recruitment and training must be placed on a fast track, and it must be done soon. And with recruitment and training must come adequate compensation as well. The *raison d'etre* of teaching is that students learn what the teacher and the society really want them to learn. But the society must be willing to put its money where its mouth is: teaching must be compensated as other critical professions are. Also, it must be genuinely respected. Our country's future truly depends on it, whether we like it or not. We are rapidly becoming a nation at risk.

NOTES

1. Welsh, P. (2001, March 4). The Party Line. *The Washington Post,* p. B1.

2. Gregorian, V. (2001, July 6). How to Train- and Retain-Teachers. *The New York Times,* OP-ED, p. A19.

3. Gregorian, V. (2001, July 6). How to Train- and Retain-Teachers. *The New York Times,* OP-ED, p. A19.

4. King, C. (2001, February 24). A Public Spanking for D.C. Schools. *The Washington Post,* p. A23.

5. Levy, H. O. (2000, September 9). Why the Best Don't Teach, A Decline in Quality That Could Soon Accelerate. *The New York Times,* p. A27.

6. Gregorian, V. (2001, July 6). How to Train- and Retain-Teachers. *The New York Times,* OP-ED, p. A19.

7. Welsh, P. (2000, June 25). Great Ones Don't Always Fit the Mold. *The Washington Post,* p. B1.

8. (1993), Minority Institutions Science Improvement Program (MISIP), The U.S. Department of Education, Proposal Evaluation for MISIP Grant Application.

9. Internet site for National Science Foundation, http://www.nsf.gov/sbe/srs/nsf96311/3sidebr3.htm

10. Internet site for National Science Foundation, http://www.nsf.gov/sbe/srs/nsf96311/3leaving.htm

11. King, C. (2001, February 24). A Public Spanking for D.C. Schools. *The Washington Post,* p. A23.

12. Zernike, K. (2000, August 24). Less Training, More Teachers: New Math for Staffing Classes. *The New York Times,* p. A1.

13. Zimmerman, J. (2001, July 11). Unprepared for Class. *The New York Times.* OP-ED, p. A21.

14. Welsh, P. (2000, June 25). Great Ones Don't Always Fit the Mold. *The Washington Post,* p. B1.

15. Furutani, W., Fujimoto, J. (1999, November 7). College Readiness Year, a Thirteenth Year of Schooling at the Community College Before Students Are Sent on to College. *The Los Angeles Times.*

16. Rasberry, Q. The Extended School: Is More Necessary Better? http://wally.uncg.edu/edu/ericcass/achive/docs/ed353657.htm

17. Ravitch, D. (2000). *Left Back.* New York: Simon & Schuster, (p. 454).

18. Romey, W. (April 2000). A Note on Social Promotion. *Phi Delta Kappan,* PDK, pp. 632–633.

19. Welsh, P. (2000, June 25). Great Ones Don't Always Fit the Mold. *The Washington Post,* p. B1.

6

THE TEACHING MODEL

A Solution for Reinventing the Teacher

The teaching model presented here for fast-tracking teacher preparation at the secondary level is based on the premise that professionals who are making the decision to teach will be well-versed in their particular disciplines, such as math, biology, English, history, and so on, and will be current in them as well. Thus the big requirement for preparing these professionals as practicing teachers inevitably must focus on hands-on pedagogy or how to teach effectively, and not on abstract discussions of pedagogy. However, along with this requirement, we must also select a content for the model because teaching the major principles of pedagogy without consistently demonstrating their clear application to a particular discipline or a content field is like trying to engage in a creative act without any medium. This chapter addresses the elements of the teaching model: basic requirements for the teacher, identifiable pedagogical principles to be utilized in communicating the content, the classroom management tactics that will allow the content to be learned, rationale for and description of the content to be used, and a training time-frame for the model.

BASIC REQUIREMENTS FOR THE TEACHER

At the heart of classroom teaching are two fundamental requirements: mastery of the subject matter to be taught and a deep enthusiasm for this subject matter. The first one is obvious—a teacher cannot teach what that teacher doesn't know. The second requirement becomes obvious only after thought. Students coming into a course often can be afraid of the subject matter, bored with the idea of having to take it, and/or uninformed as to its importance. The teacher has a "marketing" job to do.

Know the Content to Be Taught

Teachers must know their subject matter and have the necessary credentials, specializations, and/or "deep" experience in their particular field. The finest pedagogy in the world is meaningless if there is an insufficient knowledge of the subject matter to be taught. Great teaching, like creativity, does not occur in a vacuum; it requires a subject matter. The transmission of a subject matter valued by a society to its oncoming generation is the *sine qua non* of teaching.

If teachers are being asked to teach outside of their discipline or do not have sufficient knowledge in a subject area they should not accept the assignment, regardless of the pressures from the administration. Many times at the high school level, a teacher having academic credentials in one discipline is instructed to teach in a different discipline. For example, as noted by the national NEA in a radio advertisement, a history major is asked to teach math, or biology major is asked to teach either chemistry or physics. Unfortunately, this administrative ploy continues to be used in times of teachers' shortages in critical disciplines, like math. These teachers are assigned to a classroom to maintain law and order and limp through the course, which cheats both the teachers and the students. For teachers it is appropriate to know what you know, know what you don't know, and let the administration damn well know that, too.

Demonstrate Energy and Enthusiasm for the Discipline as Well as for the Students

First, teachers should verbally communicate the importance of the subject matter they are teaching throughout the course. Some students won't have a clue as to the subject matter's importance and potential—this is part of the selling job, and it should be done with great energy and enthusiasm—particularly at the secondary level. Presenting knowledge without enthusiasm, coupled with a lack of humor, is analogous to visiting a cemetery on a cold, windy and rainy day: one would rather be elsewhere and may mentally—if not actually—depart. The teacher has to "sell" the discipline, and the selling job has to go on all semester. Second, teachers need to interact with the students in an informal and welcoming way as soon as they enter the classroom, giving the students time to settle themselves and focus their attention. Such behaviors as starting to write on the chalkboard at the beginning of the period and sitting at a desk shuffling through one's notes signal that "siesta time" has arrived.

IDENTIFIABLE PEDAGOGICAL PRINCIPLES AND TEACHING TACTICS

The pedagogical principles and tactics described here are based on translations of the laboratory-based learning theories of B.F. Skinner[1] and others, a revisiting of the work of John Dewey[2] (with the subject matter left in), other writings on the subject, and the knowledge accrued from the accumulated teaching and research experiences of the authors in a minority institution for over 25 years. Each principle, tactic and technique is fully illustrated with "live" classroom examples of the subject matter being taught, as well as with computer productivity software (CPS).

The trouble with the principles comprising learning theory is that they stay that way. As Hilgard and Bower noted toward the end of their classic book *Theories of Learning,* "this is a book about learning theory, not about teaching."[3] Moreover, in large part, the learning principles that are reported have been derived mainly from animal-based research. All too often, the course in learning theories offered in the Schools of Education is taught in isolation from classroom application. Although teachers need to apply these principles to their instruction in the classroom, they usually are unable to do so. The course is completed as part of their training and the notes gather dust somewhere. Thus the translation of learning theory into classroom practice is only a hit-or-miss proposition, with the emphasis on miss.

In actuality, the teacher starts where the course syllabus or the textbook begins, and if some of the learners aren't at that point, the burden of responsibility usually falls on the learner. And the dictum "Start where the learner is" really becomes nothing more than a slogan. In practice, secondary and college teaching really begins with "start where the teacher is." At the high school level, the unprepared student often will struggle along; at the college level, this student can vanish into thin air. So, we offer translations of major laboratory-based learning principles into teaching principles.

Gain the Attention of the Learners Before Presenting Any Material

If the learner isn't paying attention, then the desired learning cannot take place. Many teachers start writing on the chalkboard or announce quizzes, homework assignments, or tests as soon as they enter the classroom. This information is usually lost because students are not completely settled in their seats. The students who miss this information in the beginning of the class eventually will discover from their friends during the class that some important announcement was made by the teacher. As a result, these students will interrupt the teacher during the presentation time to verify this information. Sometimes, these interruptions can go on and on, and end up destroying the teacher's presentation and student discussion. Teachers, therefore, must have the attention of all of the students before proceeding with any announcement or presentation. This can be done by reviewing the concepts previously learned with the assistance of the students, i.e., by asking, "what did you learn during the previous class?" This needs to be done on a rotational basis and should take no more than five minutes. The technique allows latecomers to participate as well. Also, teachers should make every attempt to write clearly on the chalkboard so that students sitting in the back can take notes without straining or making mistakes.

Recognize and Be Sensitive to Differing Knowledge Levels of Students

Students enter a classroom with diverse backgrounds. Therefore, their experiences, sensitivities, and knowledge bases are bound to be different. In this regard, Nagel, notes,

> In getting to know students well, teachers can come to know what instructional contexts are tolerable, possible, and desirable for various individuals. In knowing themselves well, teachers know what alterations in their own preferred style of teaching will be necessary to accommodate different children.[4]

For effective teaching, the teacher must first gain this information about students in a classroom. At the beginning of a course, the teacher must ascertain each student's knowledge level of the prerequisite information and basic applicable concepts. This assessment can usually be done on day one of a course by asking every student information: when and where did they take the prerequisite course, what other additional relevant courses they have taken, and their special interests or unusual skills. Based on the information obtained, the teacher can determine which student(s) will need more help. In later sessions, questions should be directed to the particular students that match these students' individual knowledge levels. Wherever possible, each individual question put to a student should be one that particular student can answer "correctly." Later, when the teacher and the students know one another better, missing an answer or having only an incomplete answer is not an embarrassment. The idea of never embarrassing a student is very important for the model.

Also, the teacher, to the maximum extent possible, must avoid the use of any kind of pretest in beginning level courses (e.g., introductory statistics, physics, and other science courses) and testing on the critical terminology in social science courses. Rather, use other non-intrusive ways of finding the knowledge base of the students. For example, an alternative way of determining the knowledge base of students for an introductory physics course would be: list the most important topics the student must know from a previous course. Review these topics during the first week of the course with the help of students by asking them questions and seeking input from them on some kind of rotation. This technique provides a reasonable way of uncovering the knowledge base of students without discouraging them from the course and furnishes an opportunity for teachers to review concepts where students may be fuzzy.

Sustain High Expectation Levels Regardless of Cultural Diversity

We are not perfect in an imperfect society. Teachers have value systems, prejudices, and predetermined notions. In order to deal with diverse student populations, teachers need to be sensitive to the needs, value systems and preconceived notions of those whom they address. First, teachers need to bring their own prejudices to the conscious level and try to leave them at home or in the hall—before they enter the classroom. Second, try not to judge students based on spoken English, especially ESL students, because these students are usually very capable. Third, raise the expectation level of all students not only by words but by deeds as well. In this regard, William Raspberry, a *Washington Post* columnist, has eloquently stated, "The critical change, though, is in expectation: on the part of teachers, of course, but also on the part of the rest of us, emphatically including the parents of these children. Any reform that fails to take that into account is doomed."[5] For example, one of the authors, in stating the requirements in an introductory sociology course, elicited this comment from a student, "Hey, I'm at UDC, not Harvard!" The response given was, "You are in a college course, and these requirements are to make sure that you do learn just as much as your colleague at Harvard—perhaps even more." Ultimately, this student turned out to be one of the highest achievers in the class. Also, teachers need to avoid making even ambiguous remarks that can be perceived as slurs.

Anchoring—Tying New Concepts to Familiar Experiences

This is an application of the principle of moving from the familiar to the unfamiliar. It is also a new "take" on the old bromide, "start where the learner is." For real learning to take place, the students must become active learners: new concepts must be anchored to the students' experiences, i.e., knowledge base. If some of the students' eyes have the glaze of a dead fish, are shaking their watches in disbelief, or are excessively absorbed in a blank notebook, then one is facing a "deactivated" learner. This is the translation of Dewey's dictum with regard to the use of students' experiences. Nagel, in the context of anchoring to students' present and past experiences states,

> Wise teachers know that they cannot "pour it in." Similarly, the substance must be understood by the students in terms of its usefulness. The "stand and deliver" process of sharing substance can go only so far. It must be accompanied by the active participation of students in experiencing some aspects of the information and in gathering, using, and sharing the details. Relate learning to your students' past or present lives.[6]

This anchoring may begin with an everyday example, or it might begin with some questions in a variation of the Socratic technique designed to find out what the students do know. The big thing here is to involve them. For example, with an abstract concept like centripetal force in a physics course, the teacher can use the washing machine in a house or a "time shaft" in an amusement park to anchor this concept. Everyone in the class usually has had both experiences. In no way is the precise meaning of the concept in physics compromised. The advantage of this approach is that students do not forget the meaning of the concept when it's been anchored in their experience. The abstract definition comes later.

Many students drop out of so-called difficult courses during the first two weeks of classes because they become discouraged when trying to complete their homework or class assignments. The teacher must avoid assigning impossible homework during this period. Rather, at the outset the teacher should assign homework from subject matter students should have learned in prerequisite courses.

For example, during the first week of the class for an introductory physics course, assign homework problems in the solutions of simple and complex algebraic equations, cross-multiplications, scientific and power-of-ten notation, and trigonometric functions, rather than problems that involve vector algebra.

Minimize Deductive Learning with Beginners in a Discipline

Deductive learning involves a teacher providing the general definition of a concept and then either the teacher or the students giving examples of it from previous experience. Deductive learning is wonderful for upper level students in advanced courses where all have a common and a sufficient knowledge base. Unfortunately, using deductive learning as a pedagogical principle often does not engage less sophisticated students in active learning, except that they probably will dutifully copy down the definition, perhaps try to memorize it, and then forget it. Although teaching in this way is seemingly less time-consuming initially and is equated to efficiency in covering the material, the presentation may or may not strike a familiar chord with beginning students. They retreat into a passive modality. They don't know enough to pursue the topic further with questions for clarification or restatements, and no student wants to look like a dummy by making a comment that is perceived by the teacher as being off the wall.

Here's an illustration of this teaching principle in action. The teacher first asks, "how many bytes on a page?" Silence reigns. Then the teacher states, "There are approximately 4000 bytes that are like characters and spaces on an $8\frac{1}{2} \times 11$ page." End of discussion. The topic has been covered, and the teacher moves on. The point about bytes will, except for a few interested students, drop into the void—even if they've written it down. When the same information is asked of the same students in a later session, the students, most often, have forgotten the answer, or will scramble through their notes looking for the answer.

Maximize Opportunities for Inductive Learning

This is an application of the principle of moving from concrete examples (from the specific and familiar) to abstract (general and unfamiliar) concepts. When an unknown term needs defining, the inductive approach is used to clarify difficult or abstract concepts. For example, through a questioning process led by the teacher, the students engage in illustrating from their own experiences, and the definition emerges—fully understood.

Using the same topic as was done for minimizing the deductive learning principle, but this time applying the inductive pedagogical principle, the instructor might ask, "How many lines, single-spaced, can you type on an $8\frac{1}{2} \times 11$ page?" The instructor can ask this question on a rotational basis and someone in the class usually knows the answer. This student might answer, "66 lines," based on personal experience and go on to say, "Also, there are 1" margins on all sides, so you can use only 54 lines on the page." Then the teacher can ask the question, "How many characters can you type in 12 point elite type on one line?" Someone in the class might answer saying, "80 characters per line." All of a sudden, someone says, "I've got the answer— approximately 4000 bytes per page." The teacher then asks the student to explain to the class how the answer was derived. This approach anchors the answer and the terminology within their experiences, and they don't forget.

Stimulate Analogical Learning

This is an application of the learning principle of moving from simple to complex and may involve either inductive or deductive learning. When we try to illustrate the key elements of a difficult concept, a figure of speech is used, such as a simile, a metaphor, or personification, to draw a parallel to a simpler and familiar situation. For example, when the concept of the evolution of human beings is looked at in relation to geological time, the time frame of 1 to 1.5 million years in relation to 4 billion years simply suggests a big difference, but not how huge the distance really is. However, an analogy, in this example, a metaphor, is first drawn with the four billion years being equated to the passage of a full day on a twenty-four hour clock. During the approximately five minutes (1.5 million years) before the end of the day, the evolution of man occurs. This example allows the time frames involved to take on a meaningful reality: students realize that human beings are really a case of "Johnny-come-lately" on the scale of geological time.

Divide Problems into Finite Steps

Every problem and/or task, whether simple or difficult, has a finite number of steps for its solution. The teacher needs to identify all these steps, especially for complex problems. For example, to calculate a standard deviation in statistics takes at least 10 steps to complete the problem using the whole-score formula and a hand calculator. When a student does not traverse all 10 steps, he or she realizes that an error has been made. The use of finite steps is not confined to problem solving in the sciences or statistics.

The same approach can be used in the social sciences and English. For example, literature is filled with infrequent terms used to convey precise meanings and emotional nuances. Unusual words and phrases are one reason that literature can transport us from the mundane world into more exciting realms. Yet there are steps that often can be used to gain the meaning of an unfamiliar word when a dictionary is not readily to hand. "The clear and brilliant morning was in striking contrast to the dark and tenebrous night." Here the unfamiliar word is "tenebrous," but the sentence in which it appears offers some assistance for deciphering its meaning. First, a contrast is being made between the morning and night: "clear and brilliant" versus "dark and tenebrous." Second, a kind of parallelism in the adjectives is used. The meaning of dark is common in weather usage and tenebrous is not being used in a deliberate redundancy but rather is supplementing dark. So it probably has something to do with a further quality of dark, e.g., murky, opaque, gloomy, possibly ominous. Third, if a Latin or Greek root is in use, that, too, can provide accuracy in meaning. To write out these steps seems laborious; for the skilled reader, they occur in a few seconds. Later, the dictionary can be checked, but running to the dictionary for every new or unfamiliar word is agonizingly time-consuming.

Structure the Subject Matter for Incremental Learning

Our experience has shown that most textbooks are organized based on the principle of incremental learning, i.e., simpler concepts, ideas, problems are presented first, and the more difficult parts follow. What is sometimes lacking is the anchoring in the students' experiences. If the anchor is missing, the sequence of the subject matter to be presented must be reorganized in such a way that student experience can be utilized so that the knowledge to be acquired is based upon it. Such was the case with a textbook used in an introductory sociology course taught by one of the present authors. In this instance, chapter 1 of the text began with an overview of sociology, filled with new definitions and the highly abstract and abbreviated formulations of time-honored theorists in the field. Chapter 2 followed with an extremely compact and abstract presentation of all the types of social research and more theory. And as if these two chapters were not enough, chapter 3 was a gallop through the concepts of culture using an historical approach, including a batch of hefty theorists in this area. So why not choose another textbook? The 12 texts that subsequently were examined followed essentially the same content organization. Since the author didn't want to be talking to herself by the second week of the course due to students disappearing, she rearranged the sequence for presenting the chapters, beginning with a quick and preliminary definition of sociology using the Socratic technique, then moving to the family, which was presented in chapter 10. From there, it was an easy jump to education, chapter 11. Using this approach allowed the students to utilize their direct experiences in these areas, and the only really big point to be grasped was the sociological perspective of these entities as basic social systems. Gradually, the transition to the more unfamiliar and abstract chapters was made after the students had built enough of an information base to handle the theory, the terminology and the inevitable definitions. Eventually, we arrived at chapters 1, 2, and 3 toward the end of the semester—with no student attrition.

Engage in Meaningful Practice and Repetition (Codeword: Drill)

Students must have a chance in the class period to use and illustrate newly learned concepts, terms, and processes. In writing courses, critiques should be done in class using clear guidelines for bringing the performance up to the "B" level. Selective corrections can be practiced through rewriting of short pieces, with students being informed where their latest effort falls on the grading scale. By keeping the first and last drafts, they have proof of what meaningful practice and repetition can do. In addition to these approaches, tests can be used as a form of practice and repetition by allowing students several makeups of similar tests until they master the concepts covered in a particular test. At this point, the concern should be with student learning rather than with worrying about the grade distribution in a class. An excellent example of this was provided by a math geometry teacher in a private school during a parents' meeting. He said, "Students will keep on taking a test until they get a 'B' in that test." This procedure assuredly illustrates the power of meaningful practice and repetition in basic courses.

CLASSROOM MANAGEMENT

In almost all classes at the secondary and college levels, students attend classes as "passive" rather than "active" learners, as pointed out by Dewey and confirmed by our own experiences in education. As a result, very few students pay attention to what the teacher is doing; most others pay little or no attention to what is going on in the classroom. Students may doze off, read, or engage in disruptive activities. This situation is made worse by teachers who regularly read from the book or their notes when lecturing and pay very little attention to student learning. In order to engage every student in the classroom in learning, the authors use the following management techniques to ensure student participation.

Assure Equal Participation

In almost all classrooms during lectures/presentations, questions are asked by the teacher/professor and answered by the same few students or sometimes answered by the teachers themselves "to save time." This approach leaves most of the other students out in the cold, and eventually they can become discouraged and drop out. The elimination of classroom dominance by a few students can be accomplished with the help of the "assure equal participation" technique. The point is well made by Nagel when she says, " In a discussion, the teacher may allow two, three, or more students to speak or respond before he or she speaks again. Students will feel important and credible."[7] What this means is that all students on the basis of some form of rotation (the technique involves the teacher utilizing the differential knowledge levels of students) are provided with opportunities to respond to questions from a teacher regardless of their particular knowledge level or the seating arrangement in a class. For accomplishing this participation, the teacher must deal with three aspects: (1) topic review and presentations need to be subdivided into segments for the purpose of assuring that each student or student team has an opportunity to contribute; (2) student input (questions, answers, comments) should be sought on a rotational basis; and (3) each student should always be addressed by name when soliciting input. This way, no student *disappears* from the class session.

Use the Textbook Judiciously During the Class

In many classrooms, teachers are either constantly reading from the book or making references to it during lectures/presentations, e.g., looking in the book and writing on the chalkboard—an activity raised to the tenth power. At the same time, the students are reading, too, and, in most cases, on a different page than the teacher. As a result, the students are asking questions totally unrelated to the topic under discussion, and the teacher then spends a considerable amount of time either discouraging such questions or disrupting the presentation by detouring to answer them. The teacher and the student are usually not in sync and are not connecting to each other. Valuable time is wasted going back and forth, and students are still confused. In sum, teachers should refrain from reading the book to students as a part of lecturing or making presentations. By the same token, during classroom sessions students need to be discouraged from opening their textbooks. The textbook is the basis for student-teacher interaction, not the substitute for it. A closed-book policy encourages both teacher and student spontaneity, the result of which is active student-teacher interaction.

Assign Selective Reading of the Textbook Topics *after* Their Introduction in the Classroom

Traditionally, almost all teachers encourage students to read the book before they come to the class. This approach is usually sound if the reading does not involve math, abstraction, and other unknown territory. However, reading prior to attending class has a tendency to cause a lot of frustration where the course is full of abstractions and unfamiliar situations. In these instances, students should be instructed to read the relevant concepts in the textbook only *after* they have been introduced and discussed in the classroom. This approach reduces the frustration that students will experience if they try to plow through the textbook presentation of unfamiliar material. Those students who habitually read through the book for topics that are going to be introduced in the classroom are either frustrated, because they cannot understand them, or acquire superficial understandings, which cannot be used in problem solving.

Many teachers become so absorbed with their own teaching that they have a tendency to ignore whether the students are learning or not. This pattern, which is detrimental for learning, is particularly true of new teachers who are themselves still learning to teach. Teachers must understand that their teaching is important and meaningful *only* if the students are learning. Students attend classes to learn, not to hear a demonstration of how smart the teacher is.

Therefore, teachers must become participant observers in a variant of anthropological research. They must balance their teaching (participation) with observing the students, which certainly entails instant reflection and rapid processing of information from the students. Participant-observation is impossible when teachers engage in "chalkboard teaching," i.e., spend most of a lecture writing on the chalkboard with their back always towards the students. In effect, teachers must engage in self-management in order to produce the necessary balance between their teaching and student learning.

Capitalize on Students' "Good Errors"

Utilization of the students' "good errors" can take place in different ways, depending on the setting and the subject matter. A common setting is when students are learning a new concept and the student makes an error in illustrating that concept with a "wrong" example. The seemingly wrong example is then used to demonstrate a key characteristic of either this or another related concept. The explanation that results is shared with all the other students. This is eloquently expressed by Nagel:

> Wise teachers learn not to be judgmental. They do not respond to their students by telling them they are wrong. They do not put down students, no matter who they are—instead they use words that can accept students' misguided ideas or inappropriate answers and ask for the thinking behind them. They can tell students that they have just provided the answer to the next question, or they can ask students to clarify opinions and facts. Wise teachers are patient. Even a "smart" remark can be accepted and shown to be a useful remark, if only the context were different. Learn to use students' ideas. Your acceptance will promote the risk-taking that allows them to become creative and critical thinkers.[8]

For example, when, in a computer training classroom, a participant is asked to define an unknown term such as "byte", typical answers could be: "a bit," "smallest unit of storage," etc. Of course, neither of these answers is correct, but these are "good errors." The answer of a "bit" from a participant allows the teacher to make a connection between a bit and a byte, and that is, 1 byte = 8 bits. The other answer "smallest unit of storage" allows the teacher to explain storage devices: A: the floppy drive, C: the hard drive, etc. After this back and forth, someone in the classroom will say that a byte seems to be character or that it is a "keystroke", and the correct answer emerges. In this manner, all students learn new terms.

Provide Sufficient Time in the Classroom for Note-Taking

We have all heard students complaining that they can either listen to the teacher or take notes in a classroom. Teachers, on the other hand, keep on insisting that students need to learn "how to take notes." We are certain that most teachers themselves have passed through this experience themselves. Quite often, teachers will be writing on the chalkboard and talking at the same time without paying any attention to what is taking place in the classroom. Sometimes, they will even erase the chalkboard before students have a chance to take notes of important details. This writing-talking technique allows minimal time even for adroit students to take notes. Unfortunately, other students just give up. Although this situation is less than perfect, many teachers have made note-taking even harder by using transparencies as a substitute for writing on the chalkboard. This latter technique does not allow any opportunity whatsoever for students to take notes, and they lose out completely on one of the tools of learning, note-taking practice.

This deficiency can easily be rectified. Teachers need to do the following: make certain that students are actually taking notes, allow sufficient time for note-taking, emphasize important points students need to be aware of, and allow time for sufficient questions to be asked and answered. Some teachers will complain that this takes time away from covering material. What teachers need to know is that in the short run they may be spending some extra time for these activities, but in the long run, they save time and will expedite an orderly progression through the course. Also, whenever possible, teachers in beginning courses should avoid passing out solutions to assigned problems; these problems need to be solved in the classroom in front of all the students for maximum learning to take place.

SELECTION OF CONTENT FOR PEDAGOGICAL TRAINING

In a teacher-training course, it becomes virtually impossible to demonstrate pedagogical principles for professionals by using a subject matter, like math, that many of them are not versed in. In this example, professionals who are expert in disciplines other than math are likely to miss the point because they either are not interested in learning math or become too absorbed in the math to pay attention to the principle(s) being illustrated. What they need to know is, "what pedagogical principle(s) do I need to use in order to teach my discipline effectively to my students?" Yet any current effort to teach pedagogy in abstraction or in isolation can only fail, as it has in the past. If pedagogy is taught in these ways, it will remain "out there," with no real value.

What then is the practical solution? Required here is another content through which to demonstrate pedagogical principles. Moreover, this "new" content must also become a valuable tool for all of the participants when they enter their classrooms as teachers. In effect, the subject matter or content must be new and valuable. By "new and valuable," we mean that none of the teacher trainees is likely to be expert in the particular content, although they may have an acquaintance with it. By "valuable," we mean content information they and their students can find extremely useful in teaching and learning right away. Hence, as they learn pedagogical principles, they will also see how these principles are applied in the rapid acquisition of knowledge of content. Based on our own teaching and research experiences over the past 25 years, the authors have chosen computer productivity software as being both new and valuable in training a content-qualified professional to become a fully qualified classroom teacher. Computer productivity software, in this model, consists of the computer operating system, as well as word processing, spreadsheet, database, and data presentation software, and the Internet.

Another beauty of CPS as a content is that it lends itself to all of the pedagogy of the model, including incremental learning, and it is well defined. And as these soon-to-be teachers will find out, computer productivity software, like the pedagogical and management principles, will be applicable to their particular discipline, be it mathematics or English. Finally, upon completion of the teacher-training program, the newly minted teachers are ready to assume their teaching assignments. With them they now carry into the classroom training in effective pedagogy, expertise in computer productivity software, and of course expertise in their own disciplines.

There is a tremendous downside for teachers who do not learn the computer, computer software, and the Internet. Teachers' lack of knowledge of computer software is compounded when the students are more knowledgeable about this tool than the teachers themselves. As a result, many teachers have a tendency not to assign meaningful homework that requires the use of the computer. Also, they stay away from students who are using computers, because they are afraid to reveal their ignorance about this increasingly important tool. In our own experiences, we have discovered that many times if a teacher can provide assistance to a student outside the classroom in an important area, like computers, students and teachers develop a strong bond. On the other hand, teachers who are not really good with CPS lose an important opportunity to bond with students and to teach them on another level because they are unable to assist students outside the classroom. In addition, teachers who do not understand the potential of computers and the Internet will not be able to integrate these tools into students' learning, and many even blame the computer or the Internet as a contributing factor for a student's failure in the classroom.

CHAPTER 6

PEDAGOGICAL TRAINING FOR
DISCIPLINE-QUALIFIED TEACHERS

A fundamental assumption here is that "great teachers" are made. To be successfully trained to teach groups of diverse students, aspiring teachers must acquire proficiency in teaching and management principles, of which one set is described in this book. The model we present here has proven very successful with both high school and college students, as well as with college faculty, but in no way should it be construed as the only model for pedagogical training.

A master teacher is at the helm of this entire training model. This teacher must, therefore, be an expert not only in the content (in this case computer productivity software), but also in the usage of the teaching principles and management tactics described earlier in this chapter.

Assuming that teachers who participate in this training model have academic credentials in the subject matter, the process will produce qualified teachers in two months rather than the traditional 18–24 months. Each graduate is proficient in the pedagogy of teaching and related courses and has full competency in computer productivity software. However, we need to point out that for the program to produce the desired results and to be beneficial to the high school, each participant must have at least a baccalaureate degree in the discipline he/she will teach. A master's degree in the discipline is highly desirable, particularly for those who will be teaching in the eleventh and twelfth grades.

NOTES

1. Skinner, B. F. (1948). *Walden two*. New York: MacMillan.
2. Dewey, J. (1938). *Experience and education*. Chicago, Ill.: Kappa Delta Pi.
3. Hilgard, E. R. & Bower, G. H. (1966). *Theories of learning* (3rd ed.). New York: Appleton-Century-Crofts, Educational Division, Meredith Corp., (p. 549).
4. Raspberry, W. (2001, February 5). No-Excuses Education, *The Washington Post*, p. A19.
5. Nagel, G. (1994). *The Tao of Teaching*. New York: Primus, (p. 169).
6. Nagel, G., p. 21.
7. Nagel, G., p. 71.
8. Nagel, G., p. 145.

7

PROPOSALS FOR REFORM

Proposals for education reform aimed at rescuing the failing public schools are not uncommon. Practically everybody has a pet reform or two. Proposed reforms range from sidestepping the public schools under various conditions, such as privatization, vouchers and charter schools, to curriculum changes in key areas, such as the reading and math programs, and the latest entry—high-stakes testing. Much of the emphasis in these proposals has been on the lower grades, specifically, kindergarten through grade eight. However, this book focuses on solving major problems in grades nine through the college freshman year utilizing two intervention strategies. One consists of specific actions to improve student performance. The other addresses actions to solve the problems confronting the public secondary schools that emanate from teacher shortages, low pay, inadequate preparation, and from public and political hypocrisy toward the teaching profession.

Our proposals for the two intervention strategies are organized as a three-tiered package. The first tier consists of proposals that are basically administrative decisions, which could be made by a superintendent and school board after consultations with the staff and constituencies being served. They are really stroke-of-the-pen decisions. Some of them will cost little money and time to implement, while others will require both. The second-tier proposals are specifically focused on teacher recruitment, preparation and pay. The third tier is composed of policy proposals in general form, which will require both money and time to achieve. With all three tiers, some form of lobbying and consensus building among the stakeholders will be needed.

Each proposal is stated first, followed by a rationale. For some of the proposals, a plan of action for implementation is presented, and anticipated outcomes are given. If the proposals presented here are implemented collectively over time, they will go a long way in rescuing the public education system at the high school and postsecondary levels.

TIER I: ADMINISTRATIVE ACTIONS

Repositioning of Algebra in the Curriculum

The first proposal is to teach algebra and its follow-on geometry courses, during the junior and senior years of high school for students not interested in majoring in sciences, math and/or engineering, in contrast to teaching them during the freshmen or sophomore years of high school or earlier. To be successful on standardized achievement tests, such as the Scholastic Aptitude Test and other college entrance and placement tests, students need English and algebra courses. In the current high school configuration, English is required for all four years in the academic track. On the other hand, only one, and, at the most, two years of math are required for many non-science majors. Typically, algebra is taught during the ninth grade, and geometry is taught during the tenth grade, regardless of the interests of students in arts or sciences. Students with an interest in science and math (2 percent in physical science and 9 in engineering),[1] by and large, will do very well on the quantitative part of achievement tests, because they continue to take math courses throughout the four years of high school, and algebra is applied regularly in all their courses. On the other hand, almost two years will have elapsed by the time non-science students (the remaining 89 percent) take standardized college entrance tests during the eleventh or twelfth grades. Because of this time lag, naturally, students have forgotten much of their algebra and geometry. As a result, they usually do poorly on the quantitative part of these tests. Often they will be diagnosed as needing developmental (remedial) courses in math during their freshman year in the college, courses which have become a tremendous drain on college resources for public colleges and universities.

If corrective actions are not taken at the secondary level, the problems of offering developmental or remedial courses in math at the college level are going to worsen, and students at the secondary level will also continue to do poorly on college entrance tests. Poor scores on the tests will require more and more remedial or developmental courses during the critical freshman year where the greatest attrition occurs. The authors, therefore, offer the following plan of action to overcome this problem:

- Ascertain the interests of students in the Arts or the Sciences with the full knowledge of parents either towards the end of the eighth grade or at the beginning of ninth grade to determine those students intending to major in math, physical science, or engineering.
- Students who show interest in the sciences (math, physical sciences, and engineering) should be encouraged to follow a rigorous schedule of math courses during their four years of high school, including taking algebra and geometry at the ninth and tenth grades.
- Students with interests other than the sciences should be encouraged to take algebra and geometry sometime during their junior and senior years. They should be permitted to take these courses earlier if they want to, once the rationale for delaying has been explained to them. These students, however, should be taught pre-algebra, introductory social science statistics (which requires pre-algebra concepts), and arithmetic if needed, during the ninth and tenth grades. In the area of arithmetic, drill the students in multiplication tables, addition, subtraction, multiplication, fractions, and decimals if that is what is needed to prepare them for algebra.

This plan of action, requiring only a minor reconfiguration of course offerings, should improve scores for secondary students on standardized tests, such as the SAT, and should reduce the need for remedial/developmental courses in math at the freshman level in the college. Ultimately, this administrative adjustment at the secondary level should free many resources for colleges and universities.

Outsourcing Essential Administrative Functions

Outsource the essential classroom support services at the secondary and postsecondary levels, if the current management cannot adequately deliver these services. The impact of poorly trained, non-caring, and insulated bureaucracies on teaching and learning in the classroom is deadly. The problem has been that poor managers usually do not know they can't manage. One management team makes a mess; the following one tries to clean it up and, in the process, creates a bigger mess. This process continues forever, and the problems never go away. We have witnessed this situation firsthand

CHAPTER 7

for many years, and it is well illustrated by Colbert King in his column of February 24, 2001 in *The Washington Post* where he quotes Superintendent Paul Vance of the D.C. Public Schools as saying, "The problems are just incredible.... We have a level of performance from our employees that is second to none of the worst things I have seen in my life."[2]

At many levels of federal and state government, where efficiency and cost saving have been major factors, agencies have outsourced their services, and the approach is working. We know, firsthand, that similar situations have occurred in colleges and universities. To improve support services for the classrooms, we propose that school systems:

- Outsource to qualified vendors such management functions as the maintenance of buildings, amenities in the buildings, care of grounds, purchasing of books and supplies, and main office functions and their staff. In this regard, the current staff should be hired for a year by the contractor, and employees' continuing employment with the contractor will depend on their performance. This decision must be made by the superintendent and/or president in conjunction with the governing board.

If outsourcing is done, it should free the superintendent, principals and other administrative staff from time-consuming administrative functions and allow them to focus more on preparation of teachers, improving student performance, and on the learning process.

Creation of a Short, Total Immersion ESL Program for Non-English Speakers

Create an ESL program for non-English speaking students to mainstream them into their educational program in the shortest period of time. For example, as reported in the *New York Times,* "More and more poor Latino immigrants often end up in schools where overwhelmed teachers have trouble instructing students who are struggling simultaneously to learn American history and English as a second language."[3] This situation, of course, is not limited to Latinos alone; many other immigrant groups are also facing similar situations. This practice creates low self-esteem for ESL students for a long time, as they continue to lag behind other students. Many just drop out. The "Total Immersion" program proposed here should last for a minimum of eight weeks.

Create a full-day total immersion program for non-English-speaking immigrant students to assure their fluency in English. As content for learning in English, develop units that teach American values and history, daily hygiene, peer relationships, and Americans' favorite dress and foods. As part of this program, initiate a "buddy" system pairing the English-language learner with a fluent speaker of English, who can later ease the transition of the ESL student to American culture and to the school's academic program.

The net effect of an ESL program will be that students will be unlikely to drop out, because they will not be forced to compete with native speakers of English until they are ready to do so with reasonable hopes of success. As a result, immigrant students will not be embarrassed by low grades in courses and on standardized tests and will build increased self-confidence and maintain self-esteem.

Constructive Use of Achievement Testing

Use national testing as a means of determining students' strengths and needs rather than for punishing communities or schools, actions that often have the effect of lowering student confidence and self-esteem. Testing must be balanced with the other two classroom activities of teaching and learning and must be beneficial to all who are being tested. The tests simply will affirm, without reforms in teaching and learning, what is already known, documented, and bad.

Surviving the College Freshman Year

Although the approaches described below can be applied to assist all students, struggling, unprepared and yet motivated, students stand to benefit the most because the suggested methods give them enough time to prepare themselves. Therefore, we propose the following survival strategies for college freshman:

- Reduce the number in each class to an ideal size of 15–20, so that students can have a meaningful relationship with their professor instead of simply witnessing a remote presence behind a microphone.
- Require courses that provide an overall balance of hands-on, field work, and physical activities that are less dependent on reading alone.
- Require two courses: first in keyboarding, and second in computer productivity software (Windows Operating System, word processing,

spreadsheet, presentations, Internet, e-mail, and database, all integrated into one three-hour course) for all incoming freshmen.

- Double the academic hour from 50 to 100 minutes for critical courses in math, science, and English in high school as well as in college.

Student Managed Academic and Recreational Activities

Assist the student population to plan and manage weekend and after-school activities to harness positive student energies. Once we consider schools as frontline agencies within communities, their roles can be expanded to steer students in the right directions. To a certain extent, the problems associated with teenage drinking, driving, vandalism and other harmful behaviors can be minimized by treating students as the young adults they basically are. Once this is recognized and acted upon, we would start seeing improvements in their behaviors right away.

Based on our extensive experience with students of various backgrounds, we offer the following strategies for handling student management problems:

- Subdivide the student population into two groups for the purpose of planning, managing and implementing activities: a group consisting of the ninth and tenth-graders, and another group consisting of the eleventh and twelfth-graders.
- Make common areas of the schools available for these two groups for weekend and after-school activities.
- Place students in charge of planning, managing, and implementing activities that do not fall within the school hours. Parental and school official involvement should be determined by the student groups, and the adults should maintain a "hands-off" policy towards student activities until and unless asked otherwise by the student groups. Some of the suggested activities could include: dance, silent auction, dress codes, food and drink preparation, movies, listening to records, fashion shows, athletic activities, aerobics, art, music, and so on.
- Translate the College-Level Semester Abroad Concept into Summer Abroad for all students, starting in the ninth grade, to culturally diverse countries. Funds for the program can be raised by school officials and students in any manner deemed appropriate by the school officials.
- Arrange for both private and public spaces for: computer workstations in the hallways for Internet access, study space for small groups, open ESL lab, special student projects, and so on.

- Arrange with the assistance of student leaders biweekly or monthly professional seminars for the whole school that focus on topics of: how to deal with school bullies and their victims, finding ways of engaging bullies in constructive ways, victims' options for diffusing extreme measures, etc.

TIER II: RECRUITMENT AND TRAINING STRATEGIES

Recruitment Strategies

Recruitment strategies need to be carried out concurrently at both the domestic and the international levels to address the grave shortage of teachers for secondary schools on both a short- and long-term basis

For *domestic recruiting,* we propose the following:

- First, recruit subject-matter-qualified personnel from industry who are either terminated because of a reduction in force or who no longer want to work for private industry. Also recruit defense personnel who have retired from active duty and who are ready for a second career. Second, train them in a compressed pedagogical model, such as the one described in this book, in appropriately equipped and staffed institutions.
- Recruit healthy and active retired teachers without impacting on their retirement benefits and pay, as has been done in New York State, and provide a period, if necessary, for updating their teaching skills before their return to the classroom.

For *international recruiting,* we draw upon the practices of the past when there have been personnel shortages in particular fields deemed critical in the United States. Such practices have involved encouraging immigration to the U.S. of physical scientists, physicians, computer scientists and nurses, beginning in the 1960s. There is no reason why this approach should not be followed in the case of teachers in critical areas. To meet this crisis, colleges of education throughout the country would have an opportunity to do a creditable job by providing compressed pedagogical training for these teachers from abroad. For international recruiting then, we offer the following strategies:

- In the short-term, the schools probably should seek assistance from private organizations to provide trained teachers who meet the following

CHAPTER 7

qualifications: have a master's degree in the discipline, are fluent in English, and are willing to be trained in a compressed pedagogical model suitable for the diverse student populations that they will face. This procedure for recruitment may require contracting with head-hunting firms, because school systems may lack the expertise for recruitment in the international market. Recently, headhunting firms have been used by school systems and colleges to recruit their super-intendents and presidents. Also, based on one author's experience, we know it is easier to recruit professionals with master's degrees in the sciences and math in the international market than in the domestic one. Public school systems should ensure recruits are appropriately trained in compressed pedagogy. Funding for recruitment and training for these teachers may be handled, in part, by new federal legislation and by existing state and local funding in the appropriate categories.

This approach would allow school systems to hire teachers for an initial period of 1–2 years before making them permanent in the school system. If the teachers do not perform satisfactorily, they can be terminated at the end of the initial trial period.

Pedagogical Training for Content-Qualified Professionals

To address the problem of the huge shortage of qualified teachers in the nation's high schools, we propose a training program described below for those professionals who have at least a baccalaureate degree in their disci-pline. A master's degree in a discipline, for those who plan to teach the eleventh and twelfth grades, is highly desirable.

- Implement a compressed pedagogical model, such as the one described in chapter 6, in colleges of education and other appropri-ately equipped and staffed institutions to meet the crisis of teacher shortages. For training a group of professionals who are qualified in different disciplines, a new and valuable content, like computer pro-ductivity software, should be selected and taught with the pedagogi-cal principles described in chapter 6. For professionals who are all qualified in the same discipline, a new and valuable content should still be used rather than their own discipline because they will be critical of the content itself and will miss the pedagogical principles being illustrated.

- The colleges of education could use this opportunity to orient their faculty to a compressed pedagogical training model to start a new program to train content-qualified professionals and to select and include appropriate aspects of the model in their own preparation of undergraduates.
- For teachers who are not content-qualified, we strongly recommend that they take the necessary university courses in their respective disciplines, because there seems to be no shortcut to acquiring knowledge in them. Nobody has invented a quick fix yet for acquiring knowledge overnight.

This proposal is in line with an observation by analyst Jay Mathews who stated, "Most educators would, I think, prefer to modify the certification process, not destroy it."[4] Also, if teachers are properly trained, it should eliminate the "cop-out" of a state-mandated thirteenth year of schooling, as proposed by administrators of dysfunctional school districts.

TIER III: LEGISLATIVE REMEDIES

We all have heard the advice and/or advertisement, "Put your money where your mouth is." If education is important and a priority and the only people who can make a difference in the lives of our children are teachers, then why not pay them what the teaching profession deserves? Business as usual in terms of current pay scales for teachers is not going to produce the results that parents seek from their public schools.

For the past 5–7 years, politicians have tried to solve the problem of low achievement scores for students by providing families with vouchers. This is a very difficult road for a number of reasons: schools are opposed to it; many parents are opposed to it; only a limited number of students can be served; vouchers do not carry enough money to afford a first-rate private school; the courts have found this approach unconstitutional in a number of states; and bad school systems persist. There is no proof that the student voucher approach is producing expected gains in student performance. In fact, recent research has found that providing vouchers is not producing significant changes in student performance.[5]

For the charter schools, Kate Zernike writes, "What is known is that, based on standardized test results, charter schools in several states have scored below, sometimes far below, the traditional public schools in the same district."[6] As the evidence mounts that vouchers and charter schools are not going to solve the problems of failing schools systems, the *New York Times* weighed in with a stinging editorial on the "for profit education movement," using Edison Schools, Inc. as the main example. Edison has yet "to find its way into the black" in spite of its claims. The premise of this and other such companies has been that they could rescue failing schools and make a profit doing it. The editorial writers note that these for-profit public schools look more and more like private schools. After pointing out that education *is* an expensive proposition, the editors conclude

> Edison's fortunes show that there is no cheap way to rescue failing schools and that the prospect of a swift turnaround and explosive educational progress was a mirage all along. The only way to improve public education is to provide every child with a bright, well-trained teacher and an orderly, well-run school. That tends to be labor-intensive—and expensive—and may never be profitable on the scale that the stock market requires.[7]

So, instead of taking steps that are detrimental to the school system that must handle the main teaching responsibilities for the vast majority of students, we should assist existing school systems and their teachers to gain competency in subject matter and pedagogy, in order to produce the desired effects for all students on a permanent basis. With this background in mind, the authors offer the following strategies:

- Provide scholarships and/or other financial incentives for those who want to teach after their graduation from colleges and universities, but who are not as yet certified as teachers.
- Reduce the burden of repayment of new teacher student loans for those teachers remaining in the system. Several approaches are possible: enhance the teacher forgiveness provisions of the loan program to minimize the amount of loan that a new teacher must repay in recognition of sustained employment as a public school teacher; protect the current loan consolidation provisions of the federal loan program to allow a lower interest rate for a consolidated loan when a student has acquired both a bank loan and a federal loan; and grant a tax credit for interest payments on student loans for those teachers who enter and remain in the public school teaching profession.
- Make the base pay for all new hires in school comparable with the average industry pay for employees with similar qualifications, such as a baccalaureate degree. One such mechanism for achieving such parity would be exempting teachers from paying federal and state income

taxes, a suggestion made by Governor Gray Davis[8] of California, an exemption, we add, should cover a five-year period. After five years, it should be possible to shift to a formula that is a variant of the one suggested below for teachers already in the system. In addition, increased pay should be provided for individuals teaching in the inner city or rural schools or where more than 50 percent of the student population meets the poverty guidelines. In districts facing a severe shortage of teachers in a given discipline, such as math, differential pay should be an option.

- For teachers already employed by the school systems, we can again use Governor Davis's suggestion. Based on this suggestion, we propose a formula that distributes the burden of the increase equitably to the federal government, the state and the local jurisdictions. The recommended formula is: reduce federal and state income taxes for teachers by 100 percent during the first year; 90 percent during the second year; 80 percent during the third year and so on. At the same time increase the pay of teachers remaining in school system every year by approximately 5 percent to offset cost of living increases during the next ten years. These cost of living increases would be separate from any form of merit or seniority pay. The formula suggested here can be amended based on the training courses the teachers complete and the use of these newly acquired skills in their classes.

- Create a federally funded fellowship along the same lines as the Fulbright Fellowship for training in pedagogy for teachers and professors on a volunteer basis. The fellowship amount should be sufficient to pay for a compressed training program as urged in this book, since it is unlikely that teachers will be able to pay for the training themselves. Such training is likely to be more cost effective right from the beginning and will be permanent because teachers undergoing the training will impact hundreds of students every year. In contrast, giving vouchers to a student may benefit that particular student, but not the entire school, and is a recurring expense.

What is proposed here is not the only way to approach the crises in our schools, but it can serve as a beginning in the alleviation of these crises. It can also serve to ignite a positive and productive dialogue among the vested parties in the education process, leading to major corrective actions in our public schools.

If no positive action is taken, then what is presented in the final chapter will happen.

NOTES

1. NCES (2000-062). The Condition 2000 of Education. *National Center for Education Statistics*, p. 150, Table 136.

2. King, C. (2001, February 24). A Public Spanking for D.C. Schools. *The Washington Post*, p. A23.

3. Canedy, D. (2001, March 25). Troubling Label for Hispanics: Girls Most Likely to Drop Out *The New York Times*, p. A-section.

4. Mathews, J. (2001, July 22). Is This Any Way to Hire Teachers?. *The Washington Post*, Outlook Section, p. B1.

5. Schemo, D. J. (2001, December 9). Voucher Study Indicates No Steady Gains in Learning. *The New York Times*, p. A33; The circumstances of the U.S. Supreme Court decision, *Zelman v. Simmons-Harris* 2002, may represent a flawed example of the voucher concept. According to the *New York Times* (Friday, June 28, p. A17), the State Legislature of Ohio State enacted the Cleveland voucher program "after a federal court placed the failing school district, where fewer than one-third of the students graduate from high school, under state control." In so doing, the State Legislature was trying to give inner city parents the same option of choice that has always been available to middle class parents. However, the money cap available, $2,250 in the Cleveland example, inevitably restricts low-income parental choice either to low-cost private schools, often religious, or to other public schools with available seats. Cleveland just happened to have a substantial number of unfilled seats in religious schools. The ruling, in our opinion, is likely to raise false expectations about what can be bought with the voucher: A high-quality private school is a big-item and has the right to refuse a child admission based on financial ability to pay, seat availability and/or academic preparation. Moreover, a first class public school in a suburb can find ways to refuse a voucher as well. So, a voucher really can make parental choice an illusion.

6. Zernike, K. (2001, March 25). Charting the Charter Schools. *The New York Times*, Week in Rev. p. 3.

7. Editorial. (2002, May 26). Week in Review. *The New York Times*, p. 10.

8. Botstein, L. (2000, September 19), What Local Control. *The New York Times*, OP-ED.

8

EDUCATION APARTHEID IN OUR FUTURE?

As the twenty-first century slides into gear, the danger signs for the public schools can be seen everywhere: in the student demographics, in the unevenness of local tax-based financing, in the perceptions of taxpayers, in the search for alternatives to the public schools, in piecemeal and underfunded public policy, and in crumbling infrastructure. Fully recognizing that these danger signs exist and that they point to very serious problems, we nevertheless take the position that public education *is* the key to the continued success of American democracy. Thus, we affirm that the system cannot just merely survive but that it must thrive. However, for the system to thrive, much depends on the degree of public support that can be mustered to provide the resources needed for adequate facilities, compensation for teachers, and meaningful teacher training to meet the challenges of the diverse population in an increasingly technological society. In essence, major changes are required if the public education system is to thrive. Creating these changes, however, depends on many forces. Among these forces are the extent to which the federal role can be expanded in public education, the willingness of federal, state and local school officials to pay adequately for teachers' work and training, the will and the ability of the school systems to prepare academically diverse student populations for full participation in American society, and the political leadership that can convince taxpayers to keep on paying for their public school systems while the changes that will rescue these systems are taking place.

The most dominant and striking trend of the 2000 Census report for education is the diversity of the population at every level of the education enterprise. This diversity will shift dramatically toward a racial mixture. In the process, the school system will witness the demise of the traditional Caucasian majority as it assumes a permanent minority position in the United States. Specifically, the numbers of African Americans, Latinos, Asians, and other racial and ethnic minorities will swell as a function of immigration and internal migration. As a result, diverse ethnic memberships will challenge school systems in handling reforms and renovations for curriculum and expansion. Where will the teachers and other school personnel come from to cope with the language and cultural diversity of students and their parents? Matters are likely to worsen if pressures for a multi-language curriculum mount, as the number of minorities increases, and the desire of the current majority to conform to English as the unifying language for instruction intensifies.

Along with diversity in the school population, school systems will most likely face the shifting contours of family composition, as the much touted "nuclear family" is partly displaced by a mix of single-parent, working-couple, and blended families coping with the pressures of income and multiple jobs. These family circumstances will require that school systems provide increased services for the children of these families and may even involve some parents in the schooling of their children.

During the last decade, the economy of the United States has prospered and, with it, the pay scales of many professions as well. The big exception has been the teaching profession at all levels, in spite of the looming shortage of teachers, particularly at the elementary and secondary levels. For example, the latest report of the *Organization for Economic and Cooperative Development* of 30 industrialized countries shows that the United States is ranked twenty-second in paying teachers and requires one third more teaching hours than do other countries. The average pay per hour for a teacher with 15 years of experience in the United States is less than half for the same teacher in South Korea.[1] What these statistics show is the incredible hypocrisy we practice with regard to teachers. We pay only lip service to good teaching; we are not willing to pay hard cash for it. If we are serious about rescuing the schools, then we are going to have pay teachers adequately. But where is the money going to come from? Local taxpayers who are presently showing signs of revolt? Cities and rural areas that lack the necessary tax base? State legislatures who are already crying poor? The only source that can truly make the difference is the federal government. Nickel and dime pay increases will not work. Teachers will continue to leave. Qualified new teachers will be reluctant to enter those schools where the need is greatest. The teacher shortage will increase. And the public education system will continue to sink.

Another major force in the education crisis is the local taxpayer. Most of the funding for public schools is derived from property taxes, a financing approach that actually places local taxpayers in the driver's seat. If middle-class parents, who are the traditional supporters of public schools, perceive they are not receiving their money's worth, they will begin looking for alternatives. If these parents are not sending their children to public schools, an increasing number of them will resist the obligation to support schools that they decline to use. The issue of paying for public schools that parents do not use is not a new one, but it would become a monumental problem to handle for county and federal officials if the numbers of parents using public schools keeps on dropping, and the number of failing schools keeps on increasing. Thus, taxpayers' revolts are a distinct possibility all across the country—particularly during board meetings and election time. For example, New York State and New York City are in a stalemate over the funding of the city schools, following a court case finding that the state was failing in its commitment to provide basic educational services to its students in the city. This controversy has escalated as the city continues to underfund its share of the costs, and the state shows little intention of bailing out the city schools. Thus the schools continue to suffer.[2]

As solid taxpayers, affluent and upper-middle-income families already have the option to move their children to the private school sector, as they feel pressure to escape deteriorating public schools. Although comparatively small in numbers, with their departure will come the erosion of leadership in support of the schools and further taxpayer resistance to pay for double schooling. Such an exodus means the public schools will be faced with an increased proportion of children from less advantaged backgrounds.

Furthermore, in addition to upscale private schools, the private sector will increasingly tend to underwrite marginal schooling arrangements, ranging from home schooling to charter schools, many with flimsy programs (already the horror stories are beginning to surface in Texas, Arizona, and the District of Columbia) masquerading as quality alternatives to the "failing public schools," as the prevailing nomenclature chooses to label them. The private sector will be split into the top extreme of quality schools for the affluent and marginal schools for those who can afford only minimal schooling, with the public school occupying the shifting sands in the middle. If the public school systems continue failing to furnish the necessary education to all children, families who can afford quality private schools will, in increasing numbers, send their children to them.

Where will the state and local jurisdictions and the taxpayers go for help? To the federal government as the only institution big enough to deal with the problem. Thus, the federal government will be faced with increasing pressure to increase its financial share of the school budget. This pressure will be compelling because of the federal commitment to subsidize the education of disadvantaged students who will amount to a larger and larger percent of the public school population. Federal involvement and therefore intervention will become a national political issue, with the likelihood that financial and performance criteria will lead to a much larger role for the federal government. This point becomes obvious, since the nation will have to opt for more participation from the single source of financial support that can deliver the huge amounts of money needed. Along with this increased financial role will come a combined push for both equality and quality in the educational offerings of the schools.

Here is the future scenario for public education in the United States. If reforms as described in this book are ignored for improving public education, taxpayers' support for public education will continue to decline, and as a result, the nation faces the grim prospect of establishing a *de facto* "educational apartheid" in the early 21st century: affluent kids in quality private schools and the rest of the kids in flimsy private arrangements and failed public schools. The consequences of not fixing the public school system will lead to a permanent and costly underclass in terms of welfare, health, and criminal justice support.

Under the right conditions, the prospect of educational apartheid and its horrible expense and injustice might galvanize public-spirited citizens and political leaders to rally behind the besieged public school system as it seeks to surmount its critical days, for it is the fallout from the lack of any coordinated public policy over time that has allowed the school systems to deteriorate.

Thus, a rescue mission for the public schools must become an overriding necessity. The sheer magnitude of failing classrooms, the crumbling infrastructure, and the changes mandated by an increasingly diverse student body pose a formidable task that must be addressed and solved. In addition, new ways of financing the system will become a problem for both political parties as they engage in debate over the reality of what constitutes "leaving no child behind." A major part of this new financing must go to teacher training and pay. This training must encompass meaningful and hands-on pedagogy utilizing current computer technology, full content-field qualification, and understanding of a diverse student population. Also, we must design constructive solutions to the 2.5 million teacher shortage, which will fill classrooms with well-paid, qualified professionals.

If there is documented evidence for reversing the trend of failing classrooms, Americans will not lightly discard their obligation to support public education. The great majority of Americans realize that education is the key to survival and progress in this increasingly competitive and technical society. They clearly understand the lack of an adequate education equals personal doom and deprivation—even if they grumble at having to fund such an education. Americans want their nation to prosper and to achieve greatness for its citizens generally. But make no mistake about it: the American dream is under duress. Achieving the American dream for all our citizens must guide the public policy agenda for the foreseeable future. Neither political party wishes to be found in default for education progress and a viable democracy for all citizens. What is required is a coalition of the political parties, education and public interest lobbies, educators, and grass roots citizen groups, to save the public school system from apartheid. The success of this coalition depends on delivering sufficient amounts of hard cash through legislation and appropriations, so that teachers are trained and paid as professionals and a fully functioning public education infrastructure is provided—regardless of the affluence level of the community in which the schools are found.

NOTES

1. Wilgoren, J. (2001, June 13). Education Study Finds U.S. Falling Short. *New York Times,* p. A28.

2. Herbert, B. (2001, January 22). Starving the Schools, It's Time for the State and the City to Play Fair. *New York Times,* p. A23.

INDEX

public education enterprise, 16
  problems, 2, 4, 16
  secondary level, 7
public education key to American
  democracy:
  challenges of the diverse
    population in . . . technological
    society, 103
  compensation for teachers, 103
  meaningful teacher training, 103
  public support, 103
  resources needed for adequate
    facilities, 103
Public Funding
  formulas, 19, 20, 23

Radical Equations, 47
Rand Corporation, 52
Rasberry, Q. 70
Raspberry, William, 27, 41, 79
Ravitch, Diane, 8, 19, 29, 70
reading, 41
  act of reading, 42
  diverse populations in school
    systems, 43
  elementary teachers, 42
  orientation to higher education, 45
  phonetic, 42
  problems, 41
  readiness process, 43
  reading . . . as a means to an end, 43
  U.S. Department of Education . . .
    25 percent . . . reads below the
    fourth grade level, 46
Reagan National Airport, 25
reform strategies, 4
rocket science, 3
Rooney, Andy, 2
recruitment strategies, 97

SAT, 93
Scholastic Aptitude Test (SAT), 55

school definitions
  a magical place, 1
  dysfunctional, 1
  frontline agency, 8, 17
  high-poverty schools, 55
  magical thing, 45
*Schools More Separate: Consequence of
  a Decade of Resegregation*, 54
schools of education
  (colleges . . .), 77
Schulte, Brigid, 47
Scientific Parallel Processing Applied
  Research Center (SPPARC),
  UDC, 32
selection of superintendents, 24
September 11, 2001 terrorist
  attacks, 4, 38
Silver Spring, Maryland, 54
Simmons, Ruth, 1
Simon, Mark, 3
Skinner, B. F., 77
Smith, Franklin, 49
Socratic technique, 80, 84
Sokolove, M., 54
Sputnik, 11
Stanford 9, 52
Stanford Achievement Tests, 51
State Education Agency for Adult
  Education at UDC, 45
State of New York, 19

teacher certification, 63
teacher quality, 62
  A-tier teachers, 62
  B- and low-grade C-tier
    teachers, 62
  Tier-C, 69
teacher shortage, 59
  "Goodbye, Mr. Chips"
    mentality, 61
teaching model, 75
  at the secondary level, 75

ABOUT THE AUTHORS

Daryao S. Khatri holds a Ph.D. in physics with emphases on mathematics and computer science from the Catholic University of America. Since 1973, he has taught diverse populations in all classes at the University of District of Columbia in the departments of physics and computer science. During his tenure as a professor and a project director at the University of the District of Columbia, he and Hughes secured in excess of $6 million in the form of 15 educational and research grants from private and public sources. The major focus of these grants was to research alternative strategies to traditional teaching that could improve the learning of minority students and hence their retention rates at the college level. Similar research was carried out with District of Columbia Public Schools juniors and seniors from two inner city poor black schools. These grants were built on their classroom teaching experiences and research findings from the grants.

Anne O. Hughes holds a Ph.D. in educational psychology and reading from the University of Chicago. As an assistant professor at the University of Texas at Austin, she worked on research projects in readiness testing and English as a second language to first-grade Mexican American children in the ghetto schools of San Antonio. Later, as an associate professor at the University of Arizona at Tucson, she held a research grant for training teachers to work with Mexican American and Indian and served as a consultant to several tribes with regard to Head Start. She served as professor, director of freshman studies, and assistant provost at the Federal City

College, part of what would become the University of the District of Columbia, and coauthored a book with John F. Hughes, *Equal Education: A New National Strategy*. She was later appointed chief development officer in charge of both private and public sector fundraising. In 1979 she began her long association with Khatri, establishing professional seminars for faculty and collaborating on research and demonstration projects for improving professorial teaching and minority students' performance at both the high school and undergraduate levels.